Ten Kids *and* A Teacher

Ten Kids *and* A Teacher

Memories from a One Room School

Frankie Beathard Rathbun

Pleasant Word

© 2006 by Frankie Rathbun. All rights reserved.

Pleasant Word (a division of WinePress Publishing, PO Box 428, Enumclaw, WA 98022) functions only as book publisher. As such, the ultimate design, content, editorial accuracy, and views expressed or implied in this work are those of the author.

No part of this publication may be reproduced, stored in a retrieval system or transmitted in any way by any means—electronic, mechanical, photocopy, recording or otherwise—without the prior permission of the copyright holder, except as provided by USA copyright law.

Unless otherwise noted, all Scriptures are taken from the Holy Bible, New International Version, Copyright © 1973, 1978, 1984 by the International Bible Society. Used by permission of Zondervan Publishing House. The "NIV" and "New International Version" trademarks are registered in the United States Patent and Trademark Office by International Bible Society.

Scripture references marked KJV are taken from the King James Version of the Bible.

Scripture references marked NASB are taken from the New American Standard Bible, © 1960, 1963, 1968, 1971, 1972, 1973, 1975, 1977 by The Lockman Foundation. Used by permission.

ISBN 1-4141-0582-7
Library of Congress Catalog Card Number: 2005908602

Dedication

To my husband, Warren, for his endless hours at the computer typing from my handwritten stories, and for his encouragement.

To my critique group who tore my stories apart and helped me put them together again.

And to the "kids," the alumni, if you please, of the Bold Springs School, who shared their memories with me,

I dedicate this book.

Table of Contents

Introduction ix

1. The Beginning of a Long Journey 11
2. Never Say Never 16
3. Ready? or Not? 21
4. Meet My New Friends 29
5. A Day at the Fair 33
6. A First Catastrophe 37
7. Trick or Treat 42
8. Bullying—An Age Old Problem 46
9. Trouble in the Outhouse 49
10. Christmas Is Coming 53
11. Visitor Unannounced 58
12. Is There a Doctor in the House? 62
13. Teacher, I'm Bored 67
14. Life after Three-Thirty 70
15. Follow the Leader 76

16. Easter in the Park 81
17. Naiveté at Its Utmost 85
18. A Lesson Learned 88
19. Bethel Baptist, The Center of
    Our Community 93
20. One Day at a Time 97
21. The Worst of the Bad 102
22. Wheels at Last 107
23. The Upside of Teaching 112
24. The End of the Ride 117
25. Epilogue: Where Are They Now? 123

Introduction

The best three years stored in my memory bank are the years, 1948-51, when I spread my wings as a brand new teacher in a one-room, one-teacher school. This book is a very abbreviated record of that adventure. The events happened, not exactly as I write about them because I can't remember all the details. Who said what and when escapes me but the stories are true. I owe this book to 12 kids, no more than 10 in any one year, who blessed my life then and continue to do so.

If I have offended anyone with my fictionalizing of facts, I beg forgiveness.

CHAPTER ONE

The Beginning of a Long Journey

If the county had not closed the school, I might be there yet.

Where? In Bold Springs, Texas.

Doing what? Teaching in a one-teacher elementary school for grades 1 through 8.

It's a strange story, one that I often muse about. It begins after my graduation from high school in 1947.

"Come stay with us this summer." My brother offers to let me live with him near Houston, hoping that I can find a job and save for college in September.

For a month, I work at a Five and Dime Store for less than $20 a week. At the end of the fourth Friday, I quit. The assistant manager accuses me of taking money from the till. After all, why else would my register check out $10 short?

Miss Pipes is an old lady, her hair twisted up in a bun, who bounces around the store all day looking for a missed particle of dust, or a can of pomade out of its place on our assigned shelves. I sense she hasn't liked me from the start.

"I didn't take any money, but you don't want me here if you don't trust me, so I won't be back Monday," I tell her and turn to leave.

"No! Not so fast. Let's talk about this. There may be some other explanation," Mr. Sanders, the manager, calls out.

I am sure that he knows I have not stolen money. I walk on out the door.

The following Monday, I am hired by Sears, assigned to the housewares department, selling everything from chamber-pots to toasters. But again I am accused, this time rightly so. Sears management deems me not aggressive enough, not productive enough, so they let me go.

They fire me.

Two days before registration for the fall semester at college. Maybe next year.

At my brother's house this afternoon a letter lies on my bed. It is from Mama.

"Be on the bus from Houston early Monday morning. We'll meet you in town. Daddy sold Old Spot to Mr. Parker for $50 and Mrs. Roberts is holding a room for you just off campus. The bus to Huntsville leaves at 8:30. You'll just have time to get off one bus, and onto the other, but you'll be on your way to college. Love, Mama."

The Beginning of a Long Journey

The word "Mama" is smudged.

I don't know whether to laugh or cry; so I do both. Getting fired is much more a blessing in my case than a humiliation.

The year at Sam Houston State is fun, but challenging. I live with two other girls at Mrs. Roberts' rooming house. Each of us has our own room, but share a bathroom. We have kitchen privileges of which only Gladys takes advantage. Warming a can of soup is about the extent of my cooking.

The hamburger stand around the corner seems to be the restaurant of choice for those of us who don't live in a dormitory. And of course, peanut butter and crackers on our closet shelf are a must for midnight snacks.

Mrs. Roberts is a sweet lady, but strict and nosey. She locks the doors at ten o'clock on the dot. We know to be in before then, or suffer embarrassment. She does not appreciate getting out of bed to let a wayward child in the door.

Nosey? We often see her reading our postcards as she brings in the mail. Occasionally she forgets and comments about something she has read. We girls pretend not to notice.

Completing my freshman year as a student at Sam Houston State Teachers College, I recognize that I don't have the $50 I need to register for the 1948-49 semesters. Old Spot put me through my first year, and the 35 cents an hour that I made working in the library helped. But I have no more cows to sell.

Ten Kids And a Teacher

On a bulletin board outside the library door, people post notices of all kinds — cars for sale, rooms for rent, even job openings. One caught my eye. "Teacher needed for a one-teacher school in Polk County. Apply to Mr. L.C. Moore at …."

I don't want the job, don't think the man would even consider me, but I sit down and write a letter expressing interest.

I am really desperate. Mr. Moore must be also. I feel sure that mine is the only letter he received, but I don't ask.

A gentle knock, then the door of our library science classroom opens. Our instructor goes to the door. A middle-aged, sandy-haired man in a seersucker suit, speaks to her. Soon, she turns to the class and says, "Miss Beathard, this gentleman needs to speak to you."

I recall a few times in high school when I was called out of class. Those occasions were not always pleasant, so I am a bit anxious about this one.

"Miss Frankie Beathard?"

"Yes sir."

"I'm Sandy Moore. I believe you wrote to me expressing interest in a teaching position in Polk County."

"Yes sir, I did, and I am." *Liar*, I tell myself.

Mr. Moore and I stand in the hallway. He asks questions. I answer as well as I can with knees knocking together and my tongue playing tricks on me.

The Beginning of a Long Journey

"There's a family down the road from the school that is willing to share its home with a teacher. I'll give you the name and address. They have a son who will be in your first grade." Mr. Moore smiles. "If you want the job, come over to my office this weekend, and we'll complete the contract. I'll drive you out to take a look at the building and community."

"Won't I need to get a temporary certificate?" I ask.

"I'll help you with that. There should be no problem," he replies. "I'll see you this weekend."

"Sure," I say. "Thank you."

The bell rings. Library science class is over, and I am on my way to a lifetime career doing what I have said I would never do.

CHAPTER TWO

Never Say Never

I will never be a teacher! I have said it a thousand times, I'm sure. All my uncles and aunts are teachers. My mother taught years ago. I guess I just want to break the cycle.

My options are few, however. A woman can be a nurse, a secretary, a waitress, a clerk — or she can be a teacher. The sight of blood freaks me out, my typing skills are pitiful and waitressing will put my customers in danger. Two choices remain: be a teacher or marry the kid down the road and have babies. Which do I choose?

On a hot Sunday afternoon, September 5, 1948, Daddy's old pickup truck, with Mama and me as passengers, rolls up in front of Miss Birdie's house in the little community of Bold Springs.

"Welcome to Bold Springs," Miss Birdie exclaims as she rushes out to greet us. "We are so glad to have you here."

Mama and Daddy, Miss Birdie and her husband exchange small talk for a few minutes.

"Make that girl behave herself," Daddy says with a grin.

"And write home often," Mama adds.

They drive off down the dusty road, leaving me to begin a teaching career in a one-room, one-teacher school. They seem to have no doubts that I can handle the task. I am not so sure.

I am there by necessity, necessity because I need a job.

Miss Birdie, a trim, reddish haired lady, who shows evidence in her face of a hard life, helps me get settled into the front bedroom. Mr. Hand, her much older husband, sits in the small living room listening to the radio. Kenneth, one of my first graders, stays close to his mother. He may be having second thoughts about his teacher boarding at his house.

Doug, their teenager, is out with the Chalker boys down the lane. Teenagers in this community have few choices of things to do, I'm told. They play baseball, pitch washers or horseshoes, or ride bikes if they have one. There are no basketball courts, no swimming pools, no cars to go the 10 miles into town.

After a light supper and a time of getting acquainted, I excuse myself to do some planning. By nine o'clock, the house is quiet. All are in bed. A good idea, I think, so I set my alarm, pull the shades and crawl between the sheets.

Today is Labor Day — no classes. The day finds me at the school building alone, examining the textbooks I will be teaching from, checking out the few library books on a shelf in the cloakroom and organizing my desk. Cobwebs and dust have collected over the summer and need my attention — the outhouses, as well. The room smells musty. I open the windows for fresh air. An old broom and some rags I find in the cloakroom are put to good use.

The thought of the responsibility facing me is frightening. How will I teach eight grades at once? Grateful for the sample schedule that the Dean of Men at my college drew up for me, I attempt to fit it into an eight-thirty to three-thirty day. My greatest fear is where to begin with my two first graders. These youngsters probably won't know an A from a B.

At the front of the room, the alphabet in manuscript is posted on cards across the top of the blackboard. Cursive letter cards spread across the inner side wall. No doubt these were tacked up when the school was opened many years ago. There are no bulletin boards to display colorful teaching aids. We have none to display anyway.

Above the left end of the black board hangs George Washington's picture. Abraham Lincoln's picture is above the right end. The American flag with its 48 stars stands in the corner. A King James Bible sits on the corner of the desk.

The building is actually two rooms. On rainy days the extra room can be used for playing games at recess and lunch periods. Large windows lining the east side will provide light on cloudy days and ventilation on warm days. In the back left corner sits a huge iron butane-burning stove. I don't look forward to the days when I will have to light the thing, but that will not be a worry for several months.

Restrooms? None. Drinking fountains? None of those either. Two outhouses stand out back, one for boys and one for girls. Thirty or so feet separate them and a wall protrudes out the front to give some degree of privacy to the entrances. I understand that drinking water will be brought from the spring under the hill. A shelf on the front porch will hold the pail of cool water. It has a dipper hanging alongside.

Walking the quarter-mile of sandy road back to my new home, I am certain of two things; one, I'm not ready, and two, I am at the point of no return.

Supper is simple, but delicious. Miss Birdie is a good cook. We chat awhile and listen to the evening news. I try to engage Kenneth in conversation. I'm sure he is as anxious about his first day as I am about mine. When I go to my room, I feel the need to write Mama and Daddy. I will write often until I meet the people of the community. Calling is out of the question. Neither they, nor we, have phones.

My journey has begun.

Confident? Don't believe it.

CHAPTER THREE

Ready? or Not?

I wake up to the deafening sound of the alarm. Surely it isn't six-thirty already.

"Lord God, walk with me today, and I will give you praise."

With that prayer on my lips, I crawl out of bed. The Hands, with whom I board, do have an indoor bathroom, so I take my turn, bathe and dress. Dresses are the accepted uniform for female teachers. Thank goodness, nylons are not necessary. The day is much too hot for stockings.

"Breakfast is ready!" Miss Birdie calls. All of us sit down to hot biscuits, sausage gravy and homemade blackberry jam.

"That should keep you until lunchtime," Miss Birdie says. "Doug, you'd better brush those teeth. Your bus should be here any minute. Lunches are on the table in the front room."

Miss Birdie is very efficient. It doesn't matter what her task is.

"Ready Kenneth?" I ask. He is sitting by the radio, listening to the Lone Ranger.

"Is it time to go?" he asks as he reaches for his book satchel and new lunch box.

We walk up the road together. Kenneth tells me about other children who will be there. "There are the Marshes now," he says, pointing to three kids coming up the side road.

At the school, the children come in one by one. I greet each one, and each of them responds with a smile and "Good morning." I suggest that they put their lunches in the cloakroom and find a desk that fits to put their supplies in. There are 10 of them — two first graders, Kenneth, and Maudine, a beautiful baby faced little blonde. Clay, a mischievous appearing curly headed pudgy kid with a winning smile is in third grade. So is James. James is hard to read. He gives me the impression that he feels like an outsider, and that there may be trouble if anyone offends him. *I will need to give him special encouragement.*

George, the youngest of the three Marsh children in the school, a quiet and thoughtful 9-year-old, and Pearline, a blue-eyed brunette with curls below her shoulder, are my fourth graders. Pearline and Maudine are sisters and are neighbors of James and Margaret. Margaret is in fifth grade, Ada Jean in sixth, Mable Clara, George's sister, in seventh, and their older brother, Bobby, in eighth.

By eight-thirty each one finds a desk that fits. I walk to the front, make eye contact with each of them and introduce myself.

"Good morning to each of you. I am your new teacher. My name is Miss Beathard and I prefer that you address me as 'Miss Beathard' rather than 'teacher,' or if you forget, 'Miss B' will do for the first few days. I will need your help, and if you have suggestions, I want to hear them."

"Miss Beathard, George and me will go get a bucket of water if you want us to," Clay says.

"Thank you Clay, that will be great, but let's wait a few minutes. Now what rules do we need, or do we need any?" I ask.

"No hitting!" Clay chimes in.

"No cussing," says George.

"Don't take stuff outta somebody else's lunch box," adds Kenneth.

"Put'em in the cloakroom and shut the door if they talk back to the teacher," volunteers Mable Clara with a glance toward Bobby.

The children seem to know more than I do about what will be needed.

"Two licks with the paddle if anyone breaks the rules," Ada Jean adds.

"Yeah!" declare the other girls in unison, except Maudine. She hasn't said anything yet. The boys groan.

"Clay and George, you can go for water now." The one dipper for all of us bothers me, although I grew up with that arrangement. I suggest that each of us bring a cup from home to use instead of the dipper.

"Now, before we take a recess break, help me with this. I notice a United States flag in this corner and a Bible on the desk. Why are they there?"

"First thing we do in the morning is say the pledge," Margaret says.

"And somebody reads a verse from the Bible and then we say the Lord's Prayer," adds Mable Clara.

James raises his hand as he says, "We sing that song, you know, 'My country tis'."

"He means 'America'," Bobby interrupts.

"Then that is the way we will begin our days. Now while you take a break, I'll put your textbooks on your desks. When I ring the bell, it will be time to come in."

In a flash, the boys are out the door with the ball and bat. The girls take the jump ropes. Those, and a large rubber ball, are the sum total of our recreation equipment. We do have two swings and a see-saw on the school ground.

I get the textbooks on the desks quickly. On the board I print the first two lines of "Humpty Dumpty," then go out on the porch to observe the children. The girls are hovering around little Maudine like an eagle over its eaglets. Their assumed task is to teach her how to jump rope.

The boys are engaged in a version of baseball. James, at bat, has two strikes against him.

"If we had a pitcher who could pitch, I could hit the ball," he yells.

George, who is pitching, opens his mouth to reply, but notices that I am watching, and restrains himself. I think it may be a good time to ring the hand-bell.

After the books are examined and placed in the desks, I give grades three through eight a sheet of arithmetic problems appropriate for their grade levels. They work on those while I work with the beginners. We recite several nursery rhymes and then "Humpty Dumpty." I explain that I have written the rhyme on the board.

"Let's read it together, okay?" Worried expressions turn to surprise as I point with my long pointer stick to each word as we say them. "Wow! You can read. Your first day in school and you are reading!"

Like a child with a new puppy, big smiles of excitement and disbelief spread across their faces. We "read" several times, then use flash cards to recognize the letter B,b. They go back to their desks with a sheet on which I have printed each one's name several times. I instruct them to trace their name, then print it without the pattern.

Whew! First graders taken care of for a while.

The older children complete the arithmetic sheets, and read the first story in their readers. Using questions that I have prepared, we discuss together the various stories. This activity helps me recognize comprehension skills, ability to express ideas, which ones are not able to complete the assignment, and their levels of enjoyment or boredom with reading.

Lunchtime is fun. Some choose to eat inside, others choose the shade of one of the trees on the school ground. I turn the classroom radio on to hear the noon news, then go outside.

"Let's play dodge ball!" shouts Bobby. "I'll be in the middle."

"I will too," calls Clay.

The others form a large circle. I join them. Margaret throws the rubber ball as hard as she can, aiming it at Bobby, but it misses. The guys in the middle pretend to be statues, spreading their legs and arms in all directions. Kenneth throws the ball directly at them, but the "statues" crumble to the ground. The ball whizzes by and into the hands of George. Bobby turns his back to his brother and bends over with his head between his legs and laughs at George. His backside is a promising target, so George lets the ball fly. It reaches its target before Bobby can jump out of the way. We all roar with laughter, while George takes Bobby's place in the middle. The lunch hour ends too soon.

The afternoon goes smoothly and fast. The older ones examine geography and science books. The younger ones draw pictures of their families with their new crayons, then tell us about each of them. Kenneth draws his dad sitting in a rocking chair on the front porch while his mom washes clothes on a washboard. Maudine's picture is of her grandpa on his tractor.

Mr. Hand's old truck rattles into the school yard signaling the end of the school day. Mr. Hand's truck substitutes for a school bus for the children who live north of the school, too far to walk.

"Any homework?" Margaret asks.

"Your homework for tonight is simple," I reply. "Take all your books home and cover them. Grocery bags make good covers. Thanks for your help today. I'll see you tomorrow."

"But, Miss Beathard, our teacher last year always had somebody sweep the room and somebody else empty the pencil sharpener and the trash can," Mable Clara says.

"Oh my! That has to be done, doesn't it? I'll tell you what; I will take care of it all today, and we'll ask for volunteers tomorrow."

In the quietness of that hot afternoon, I sit at my desk, meditating on all that has happened this first day, and pray, "Thank you, Lord. You know, I think I'm going to enjoy this journey."

1948: An angelic bunch...Agree?

CHAPTER FOUR

Meet My New Friends

In a rural community everyone knows everything about everybody — not always a good thing. But I see Bold Springs full of beautiful people, beautiful from the inside out.

A strong and inspiring lady, Miss Birdie does not know the meaning of the word "vacation." She has Kenneth and Doug and a much older husband to care for. He is not able to work, so she arises early and makes fried pies from dried fruit. When Kenneth and I are off to school, she loads her basket of pies and drives to the café in town where they are sold in short order.

You'll never hear her complain, and she revels in the pleasure she gives others. Miss Birdie spends her spare moments writing to Junior, her 18-year-old son in the Army.

Blanche and Edker are an interesting couple. She, always prim and proper and dressed fashionably, is a homemaker. Hospitable and social, she either is preparing for guests, or taking food to someone in need. Edker raises Beagles and spends nights chasing his dogs through the woods on the heels of a fox. He manages the pump-station by day, one of the few men in the community who has a consistent income. Their daughter, Nellie Jo, lives and works in Houston.

Bobbye Lee boards in town while going to high school. Friday afternoons, (or Saturday mornings, if she has plans for Friday night in town) Tub Rogers, her dad, drives into Livingston to bring her home for the weekend. "My doll is coming home," he says with a gleam in his eyes. Tub raises cattle and feed crops.

Faye, Tub's wife, is a quiet lady. She keeps her emotions under cover, except when Tub doesn't get to the table on time for meals. Faye has her way of doing things and there is no changing her. When she is busy and Tub suggests she do something, her common reply is, "I can't milk but one cow at a time." The job gets done, but according to her schedule. And don't make the mistake of asking Faye about her weight or age. She'll tell you in a flash, "That's none of your business."

Monday is wash day for Faye. Although she can afford a washing machine, she prefers her way. A fire is built under the old wash-pot after filling it with water and homemade lye soap. The clothes go in, she swishes them around with her long paddle until she knows they are clean, and finally, after rinsing, Faye hangs them on the clothesline to dry in the sunshine. It is a Monday morning ritual and nothing short of a death in the family interferes. But Faye has a soft side; she will do anything to help a neighbor.

Up the hill from the Rogers, sits Big Mama's house. She is Tub's widowed mother. Eva, her widowed daughter, lives with her, and theirs is the place to go if hungry or needing an emotional lift. No one has been able to figure how those two ladies can always have a complete meal ready in the old safe for anyone who comes by at anytime.

So many others I could introduce you to, but I'll stop with Mr. George Grimshaw and his wife, Donna. They are Faye's parents. Mr. George, as everyone knows him, involves himself in everything good that happens in the community. If a bull has to be loaded into a cattle trailer, a hog needs to be butchered, or someone needs to be taken to the hospital, Mr. George is there to help. He is a school trustee, a deacon in the little Baptist church across from the school, and the caretaker of the cemetery beside the church. He can be reached at home only at breakfast or supper time. As long as the wheels of his pickup will turn, Mr. George is on his way to somewhere.

On the other hand, Mrs. Grimshaw is a homebody. Church on Sunday is the sum total of her socializing. She is gracious to those who drop by, but we all know not to go between one and two o'clock, her nap time. She lies down on the floor in front of the screen-door with her pillow and a cardboard fan that advertises the local funeral home. She becomes very annoyed if anyone walks up onto her porch while she is resting. After her nap, she sits in her rocking chair on the porch, snapping beans, shucking corn, crocheting, or whatever else she feels she needs to do while watching the "world" go by on the sandy road out front. Not very exciting probably, but Mrs. Grimshaw knows more about what is happening in our part of the world than any of us.

"Preacher Hand went up the road. Wasn't gone long, guess he went to check on old man Baker. Tom Marsh took a load of squealing hogs to the auction. Didn't see him come back. Guess he stopped at the feed store."

These are the kinds of events Mrs. Grimshaw reports to George at night. Of course, if the truth were known, Mr. George probably helped Tom load those hogs.

These and many more have become my good friends at Bold Springs. Each has his or her own eccentricities, but all are caring, beautiful people.

CHAPTER FIVE

A Day at the Fair

We at Bold Springs school, all eleven of us, became a family within days. For the teacher especially, learning is a top priority. I have so much to learn. But having fun together has become a close second. We take advantage of every opportunity to make learning and fun the same.

Kid's Day at the county fair is my first exciting challenge. All of us pile into Mr. George's pickup for the 10 to 15-mile trip to the fairgrounds.

"Now children, you are to sit flat on your bottoms until I park the truck and tell you to get out," Mr. George says with authority.

"Yes sir," they reply. The older ones know there will be consequences if they don't. Mr. George is their best friend, but he can be their worst enemy if they disobey.

At the fairgrounds, each is given tickets for the carnival rides. I assure them that they can have hot dogs and lemonade later, cotton candy and maybe ice cream if there are no problems. The boys and Mr. George head out toward the tractors and farm animals. The girls and I take in the crafts and food displays.

"Look at those quilts! Miss Beathard, which one do you like best? I like the one with butterflies," Pearline exclaims.

"The judges must have, too." I point to the blue ribbon attached to the corner of it.

My choice really doesn't matter. So thrilled with all she is seeing, Pearline forgets her question.

"Oh my gosh! How did some lady make that birthday cake look like a castle?" Margaret asks.

"My aunt Beulah could do that," Ada Jean says. "She made me a cake with a doll in the middle."

"Could you eat it?" A doll in a cake is more than 9-year-old Pearline can imagine.

"We ate the cake part, but not the doll, silly."

"Let's check out the rides," I suggest. "When our tickets are all gone, we'll get something to eat."

"Are you going to ride, too?" asks Mable Clara.

"No, no, I meant when YOUR tickets are gone. I'm going to watch."

The older girls take little Maudine by the hand. If she doesn't want to get on a ride, they can bring her to me.

Later, the boys show up. "I dare you sissies to get on the Tilt-a-Whirl," Bobby says with a twinkle in his eyes. He speaks as one who has already been on it.

Of course, that dare is all the girls need. They climb aboard, all but Maudine. With screams and laughter and an occasional groan, they twirl back and forth, side to side. I'm sure the attendant is allowing the ride to last longer than usual. Finally, it stops and the girls climb off.

"Goody, goody, we did it, and it was fun," the girls shout to the boys.

I wonder if the boys notice how quickly Margaret has turned away. She's lucky that her tummy is empty. Her face is pale. I know exactly how she feels. I have been on a Tilt-a-Whirl myself — only once.

Mr. George walks by. "I've lost James," he whispers.

"Let's take the children over to the concession stand, and while they are eating, you and I will look for him. I'm sure he is fine; probably he has found someone to listen to his tall tales. For an 8-year-old, he's full of them."

Everyone orders a hot dog and something to drink. Mr. George buys bags of potato chips for them and directs them to picnic tables nearby.

As I stand in line to pay for it all, I feel a nudge on my backside.

"Miss Beathard, we sure won't lose you in this crowd with that dress on."

Yes, it's James admiring my bright purple dress. He doesn't know that he was lost.

With cotton candy all over our faces, we arrive back at school just as Mr. Hand drives up in his "school bus."

"Thank you, Mr. George, thank you! We had fun, fun, fun!" All 10 are clamoring at once.

"If these wheels keep turning, just maybe we'll go again next year," Mr. George replies. "I had fun, fun, fun, too."

"Any home work, teacher — I mean Miss Beathard?" Bobby asks.

"No, not tonight, but be ready to write about your day at the fair tomorrow."

The children never question about who paid for their day. It is just one of the perks that the county superintendent provides for the rural schools from his budget.

CHAPTER SIX

A First Catastrophe

I ring the bell at eight-thirty — time to take up books. The girls run in. The boys saunter to the porch and stop for drinks from the bucket of yesterday's water. Clay, sure that he has left a few drops in his cup, cannot resist slinging his cup toward George. George yells, "TEEE-CHER!" Just as quickly, both boys rush into the room laughing. George wipes his face on his sleeve. I frown a puzzled frown, then smile. Just being boys, I think.

After the pledge and "America," we say the Lord's Prayer — our usual introduction to the day's work. Reading exercises go well. Homework papers are turned in.

"James, I don't seem to have your story. Did you write one?"

"I can't find it. I musta left it on the kitchen table."

"He can just stand up in front and tell us his story, can't he, Miss Beathard?" chirps in Clay.

"That is a good idea, Clay," I reply. "And you can tell yours next."

Clay looks worried. "No, not me! That is NOT a good idea."

"Kenneth, what time is it?" I ask. The first graders are learning to tell time.

"Uh, the big hand is on 12 and the little hand is on 10. Ain't that recess time?" asks Kenneth.

"Good job, Kenneth. You are correct. Put your books away and you may go out."

"What? Can't we go out, too?" asks Margaret.

"Everyone can go out. Whose turn is it to get fresh water from the spring?"

"Me and Pearline," says Mable Clara. She grabs the bucket and off they run. They don't want to use more recess time than necessary fetching water.

Soon they are back and they join the remaining eight who are playing "Annie Over," four in front of the building and four in back. Those in front yell "Annie" and one throws a ball over the building. Those in back cry "over" and watch as the ball comes across the roof. Someone catches it and he and his team have to run around to the front. Whoever has the ball has to throw it at someone from the other team. If he succeeds, the person hit is out of the game. When the team in front realizes that the ball has been caught, they run to the back, trying to avoid being hit.

A First Catastrophe

Sitting at my desk checking papers, my ears are tuned to the activity outside. Suddenly the laughter turns to screams. Someone is hurt. I have always known that there would be mishaps or emergencies sooner or later. I hoped they would come later.

Running around to the back, I see a gang around Pearline, and another around Clay. The screams are coming from Pearline. Her nose and lips are bleeding and swelling. She is leaning forward to let the blood puddle on the ground.

I look at Clay. He is rubbing his forehead, but he says, "I'm OK, Miss Beathard. We runned into each other coming round the corner." Clay's head is like a brick. No wonder Pearline is bleeding.

Margaret rushes to me with a box of tissues. I clean Pearline's mouth as well as I can. The bleeding stops, and we put a cold, wet pack of tissues over her lips and have her rest her head on her desk. Mecurochrome and Band Aids are all I can call my emergency kit.

Neither is suited for this crisis. Clay has a big bump above his eye, but it is obvious that he is enjoying the attention from his classmates.

Ada Jean whispers, "Miss Beathard, you need to sit down."

I am trembling. My stomach is queasy. I want it to be time to go home, but it isn't. As I sit at my desk, I talk to myself. *Get it together. You are the adult here.*

"Mable Clara, take Maudine and Kenneth to the back of the room and listen to them read, please.

Everyone else, turn to the next page of your arithmetic books, read the instructions and complete as many problems as you can. If you need help, come ask. We'll check them after lunch."

Noon comes quickly. Everyone grabs his lunch and heads for the shade under a tree — all except Pearline and me. We nibble at our sandwiches on the steps of the porch. While the boys play tree tag and the girls play hop-scotch, Pearline and I play tic-tac-toe using sticks in the sand in front of the steps.

The afternoon goes as well as we can expect. Pearline falls asleep with her head on her desk. When Mr. Hand comes, I explain what happened.

"I'll get her home safe," Mr. Hand assures me.

He puts Pearline in the front seat with him and drives off. I wonder if her mother will take her to see the doctor, but not once do I think of a confrontation with a parent. Things happen. Parents accept that as fact.

I trudge through the hot sand to my sanctuary, glad that I survived the trauma. Surely nothing worse can happen. Or can it?

A First Catastrophe

Hey! Don't bother us. We're eating.

CHAPTER SEVEN

Trick or Treat

Halloween in the Bold Springs community involves the entire population. Everyone, young and old, gathers at the school; none of this going from door to door asking for handouts. In the first place, neighbors live too far apart, and besides, the traditional chili supper is better than anything we can think of.

The three school trustees, Mr. George, Tub Rogers and Mr. Wainright, take care of the chili-making. Tub drives up with an iron wash-pot in the bed of his pickup. Their wives have put together ingredients for a pot full of spicy chili. Tub, with help from the others, unloads the pot and places it on an open fire that the men have started. The chili-makings are poured in and the main course begins to simmer.

Trick or Treat

The men bring tables from the little church across the road to hold the pans of cornbread and bowls that families will bring later.

Tub's wife, Faye, and her friend, Blanche, come to help — mostly to supervise.

They mark the empty classroom floor for a cakewalk and set up a record player. A tub of water with apples floating in it is placed on the porch.

By six-thirty, vehicles line the road out front, and the school yard fills with chattering grown-ups and squealing children. Tub gives one of his ear splitting whistles to get everyone's attention.

"Welcome to the party," Mr. George says in his loudest voice. Mr. George has the respect of everyone in the community. We all stop to listen. "Let's ask Preacher Hand to say grace."

It seems to some of us that Mr. Hand talks to the Lord an unusually long time, but all heads bow until Mr. Hand finishes, then noise resumes. Mr. George has to get our attention again.

"We'll form two lines, one on each side of the chili pot. Get your bowl full, grab some bread and a soda water, and enjoy the evening. After you eat, there'll be a cakewalk in the school and apple bobbing on the porch. Oh, I almost forgot," Mr. George adds. "You kids will wait until the old folk go through the line. If there is any food left, you may eat." Mr. George chuckles as he makes the announcement.

"No! no! no! It ain't fair!" Screams come from all around the yard.

"Just kidding," Mr. George says, "but do remember your manners. Take your turn."

The chili is hot and spicy, just the dish for a cool October evening. Seconds are in order for those with strong stomachs.

The older youngsters know the routine. When Miss Blanche and Miss Gladys head toward the building, they know the cakewalk is about to begin. Several ladies have brought cakes to be won. A circle with 10 numbered spots has been drawn on the floor. One person stands on each number.

"The person on number five when the music stops will win this one," Miss Blanche announces as she holds up a pretty pastel-frosted cake.

Miss Gladys starts the record. All 10 march to the tune of "Stars and Stripes Forever," each stepping briskly to the next number. Miss Gladys keeps her back turned to the group so that no one can say she favors one over the other. Suddenly she stops the music.

"It's mine!" Doug yells. He is standing on number five. "Cloyce, you can take my place." Doug takes his cake and goes out to find his mother.

"See what I won, Mama. Will you hold it for me? I want to try bobbing for apples."

Back in the classroom, Miss Blanche holds up a cake shaped like a ghost. "Nine is the lucky number for this one."

The music begins. Excitement fills the room. The onlookers are having as much fun as those marching. Each person who wins a cake chooses another to take his place in the circle.

While the cakewalk continues, the brave ones duck their heads in the water to capture an apple with their teeth. Clay comes up with one. "It's harder than you think," he says shivering. "I don't know if it's worth it."

Out around the smoldering fire a group has gathered. Miss Birdie begins singing the words to "A Bicycle Built for Two." That is all that is needed to prompt the others to join in. Everyone knows the words, and most even know the tune.

The lights go out in the school building. That is Mr. George's signal that the party is over — time to go home.

"Tub and I will take care of the clean-up in the morning," Mr. George says. "Happy Halloween to you all."

"Don't let the goblins get you," Clay yells.

My guess is that most are thinking less of goblins and more of Alka Seltzer at this moment.

CHAPTER EIGHT

Bullying—An Age Old Problem

"Whatcha got in the box, Margaret?"

"You don't need to know, Clay Lawrence. Nothing that you'd be interested in anyway," Margaret grumbles.

"Huh, maybe I would," Clay says. "Let's see." Clay lands a fist on the near-side of the box, knocking it from Margaret's hands. Paper dolls scatter all around in the dirt.

"You're right, I'm not," Clay laughs. George joins in the fun. Kenneth stands at a distance with a surprised gaze, probably not knowing what would be a safe response.

Margaret's eyes fill with tears. Her face turns red with anger. With rage in her voice, she screams, "Clay Wallace Lawrence, you pick up my paper dolls!"

Bullying—An Age Old Problem

What I am hearing and what I see as I come out onto the porch is so out of character for Margaret. Ordinarily Margaret is meek, never drawing attention to herself. It's frightening to see her in such an agitated state. "Clay, you go to the corner of the building and stand there until I give you permission to move. I'll hear from you later."

"Margaret, pick up your paper dolls and come into the classroom."

"No! I won't pick them up. Clay put them there. He can pick them up," yells Margaret, her voice quivering.

The other girls stand by, no doubt wondering what is about to happen.

"I'll pick them up, Miss Beathard," Pearline says.

"Thank you, Pearline. Margaret, come into the classroom with me."

Margaret turns toward Clay, gives him a wicked glare, then inches toward me.

I take her hand and proceed to lead her to her desk. I wonder how her morning has been at home. Margaret's mother is emotionally ill to the extent that she cannot take care of her children at times. Margaret's little brother had fallen into a pail of water and drowned. Her dad has to be away at his work, and it falls to Margaret to see that her little sister is fed and dressed before leaving for school herself. She is such a little girl to have that much responsibility. I walk to my desk and sit down.

Should I bring the others in, or wait awhile longer. And what shall I say or do to Clay?

I know without asking that Clay initiated the conflict, and on purpose. Clay is like that, and James and Margaret are his favorite targets. Clay is being reared by an older aunt and he is accustomed to being the center of attention. I know nothing about his mother and father. I'm not sure that he does either. Most adults in the community call Clay, "Sugar," because they seldom hear him called anything else.

Moments pass as I contemplate what to do next. Then I hear Margaret sobbing. I look up. She is running to me.

"I'm sorry, Miss Beathard, I'm so sorry. I shouldn't have done that. I'm so sorry. I sassed you, and I shouldn't have done that. I'm so sorry." She sobs violently as she repeats those words over and over.

Tears rush to my eyes, too, and I put my arms around her, stroking her head, patting her back, and holding her trembling body close.

"It's okay, Margaret. It's okay. Dry those tears and let's go on with our day's work." I hand her tissues from my desk. "Wipe your face and take the bell out and ring it for me. And tell Clay the teacher said he could come in. Can you do that?"

"Yes, ma'am," Margaret whispers.

Margaret wipes her face several times, gives me a smile and goes out with the bell in her hand.

What a brave young lady.

CHAPTER NINE

Trouble in the Outhouse

Mondays come around often during the school year. For some reason we don't notice their regularity in the summer months. Are the students tired from weekend activities? Or maybe they are so rested that they hate the thought of lessons and homework and having to get along with all the other kids and especially with the teacher.

I have to admit that I'm not always super thrilled when the alarm clock rings on Monday mornings either. Why hasn't someone thought of having the school day begin at ten on Mondays?

Kenneth and I mosey along the sandy road. The sky looks threatening. Thunder rumbles in the distance. Recess breaks will likely be spent in the adjoining room today. That will not bother the girls. They enjoy Pickup Sticks, Jacks and Chinese Checkers. What about the boys? Maybe a game of marbles in the far corner. They will think of something, if only pestering the girls. That's always a favorite activity and they are masters at it.

The other nine students arrive barely on time and come in reluctantly. After all, it is Monday, and I understand.

Suddenly, the sky opens up — a gullywasher in a matter of minutes. Earsplitting claps of thunder and frightening streaks of lightning interrupt our class activities.

"I'm scared. I want to go home," little Maudine cries. She covers her head with her opened Dick and Jane primer and closes her eyes. Kenneth sticks fingers in both ears to shut out some of the sound.

Electrical storms are not my favorite gift from Mother Nature either. In fact, I am downright petrified, but I have to remind myself. *I am the adult here. Calm down.*

Each grade has a class assignment written on the chalkboard. I give instructions to the first graders and ask Margaret and George to help them if they ask for help. Ada Jean, Mable Clara, Bobby and I work with percentage and use of decimals.

"May I be excused?" Mable Clara asks. That means she needs to go to the toilet. The rain has slacked a bit.

"Yes, take my umbrella, and be careful. The trail may be slippery."

"Bobby, if Farmer Brown has a horse for sale for $185, but because you are his good neighbor, he'll give you a 25% discount, how much will you pay for the horse? Show us on the board."

Bobby grins and starts to the front. He seems sure that he knows how to get the answer. But before he can write the first number, a bloodcurdling scream penetrates the closed windows.

It is Mable Clara obviously in distress. I rush to the window. I expect to see her lying in a heap in the mud with a broken arm or leg. Instead I catch a glimpse of a frightened young lady, her arms flailing the air, running toward the building, yelling "They did it! I know they did it!"

Mable Clara dashes into the room. I can't decide if she is more frightened or more angry.

"They did it, Miss Beathard! I know they did it."

"Did what?" I ask.

"Put that nasty-looking varmint in the girls' toilet!"

"What varmint?" Bobby and George ask at once. They look so innocent.

"You know what varmint — that armadillo!"

It is all I can do to keep a straight face. The boys laugh out loud, the girls restrain themselves with a little smile. No doubt they realize that any one of them could have been the victim. My stern gaze quiets each of the boys.

"We ain't guilty, Miss Beathard. He probably found the door open and went in to get outta the rain." That is Clay's explanation.

"And I guess he shut the door after he got in." Mable Clara says.

Giggles from the girls.

"Whether you did or didn't, Bobby, you and George, go get him out of there."

"He's gone!" James is looking out the window. "He's runnin' down toward the spring," he announces.

"Now can Margaret go with me back to the toilet?" asks Mable Clara.

I watch through the window. The girls ease the door open in position to run if they need to. Both look in. Finally Mable Clara enters and closes the door. The toilet is a one-holer, so Margaret waits outside.

We may never know for sure how the armadillo got into the outhouse, but I think it is a safe bet that two or more of the boys know.

Oh well, all's well that ends well and besides, Mondays need a little excitement.

CHAPTER TEN

Christmas Is Coming

Christmas is coming! Christmas is coming! We are excited. My favorite of all holidays is Christmas. Memories of Christmas past flood my mind: the year Santa left me a Shirley Temple doll, the well-used bicycle that my little brother found outside the front door — his first bike, roller skates another Christmas. There were the evenings when neighbors gathered around Mama's piano to sing carols. My older brothers made efforts to be home for the day. The holiday is special.

At school our big window panes are plastered with stars and candles and paper Christmas trees. All of our lessons relate to the seasons. In arithmetic class we pretend to shop. Symbols of the season make up our spelling lists. We write about traditions, and we sing.

"I know a Christmas song, Miss Beathard. You want to hear it?"

"Yes, Maudine, please sing it. Come up front so we all can hear."

Maudine, her head down and in a quiet voice, sings "Up On the Housetop." The class applauds. She lifts her head and smiles, her big blue eyes glowing.

"Can we sing with you?" I ask. Not waiting for her answer, all the kids chime in.

George, Clay, and James belt out their version of "Santa Claus is Coming to Town." Cheap entertainment, but we are having fun.

A community Christmas service and tree for the children at the little church across the road is tradition. The teacher is expected to have her pupils present the Christmas pageant. When I was told about this, I knew it might be a challenge. We need all the parents to commit to get their children to the church on the scheduled Friday night.

"Let's see. We'll need at least 10 characters," I say.

"Well, we have 10 kids," Ada Jean reminds me. "We can do it."

After some thought, I'm ready to assign parts.

"Maudine and Kenneth, you can be Mary and Joseph. Margaret and Pearline, you will be angels."

Bobby and George are quick to volunteer to be wise men.

"But you need three, so I'll be a wise man, too." Clay says.

Christmas Is Coming

"Okay, Bobby and George and Clay will be our three wise men. Now all we need are some shepherds."

Ada Jean, Mable Clara and James are unassigned. Three shepherds will be enough. I ask each of them if being a shepherd in our program is okay. James is not too gung-ho about coming down an aisle with two girls. The girls aren't too keen on pretending to be men, but all three agree, "just for the teacher."

We practice for days in the classroom and over at the church. Each character knows exactly when to enter and what to do. The few speaking parts are perfected. I am the narrator.

Friday night, December 17, finds the community gathered in the church. Carols ring out. The minister prays. The lights go out. A few candles shed light on the podium. The light at the back entrance where the magi are to enter is still on. A Christmas tree in the right front corner provides some illumination.

The pianist begins playing quietly "O Little Town of Bethlehem," and I begin the story recorded in the Bible. Mary and Joseph take their places. Mary lays her baby in the manger. The shepherds appear from the side door accompanied by the angels. All three shepherds turn to the angels, gasp, and cover their faces with their hands to show fear, just as they had practiced.

"Be not afraid, I bring you good news," exclaims Pearline.

"Today a Savior is born. He is Christ the Lord," Margaret continues. "Go to Bethlehem and find the baby in a manger."

The shepherds gather around Mary and Joseph. Everything is going well. The pianist switches to "We Three Kings," and I read from Matthew. This is the cue for the wise men to enter from the rear entrance. I look back. My "wise men" are goofing around at the door, not listening. Seconds later, I catch George's eye.

Quietly they start down the aisle — acting like wise men? No! They are tossing their gifts in the air. I wilt. They grin. Lucky for them, and for the teacher, when they reach the first pew on which people are seated, they change into authentic "wise men." They lay their gifts beside the manger.

The pianist plays, and the children sing "Silent Night." The congregation joins in. The lights are turned on.

I breathe a sigh of relief. It's over. We did it.

Almost instantly sleigh bells ring. The little ones jump and squeal as the back doors swing open and Santa dances in with his "Merry Christmas, ho! ho! ho!" The crowd goes wild. The adults, including me, wonder who is behind that beard. The children know full well. It's the man from the North Pole with a bag full of gifts.

Santa begins his task. "Here's a big box. I wonder who it is for. Oh yes, the tag says 'Jimmy' but I don't think he's here."

"Yes, I am," shouts a little guy no bigger than the box, rushing to the front.

"What do you say to Santa," a mom calls.

"T'ank you," and he's gone, struggling with the big box, like an ant pushing a chunk of bread.

"I think this baby wants to go home with Emily," Santa announces as he picks up a curly-haired doll.

"That's me!" shouts a little girl sitting on her daddy's lap.

When all the packages are given, Santa exits with his "Merry Christmas to all and to all a goodnight."

Every child has received a gift. The trustees provide an especially nice gift for each school pupil, and parents bring gifts for their preschool children. Everyone is going home with a bag of candy and an apple and orange.

This night for some will be the nearest thing to a Merry Christmas they can expect. For me, it is the beginning of a two-week visit with my family. Mama and Daddy have driven over to take me home.

CHAPTER ELEVEN

Visitor Unannounced

"Miss Beathard, James and Kenneth are fighting! You'd better come see!" Maudine runs into the room as if she were about to be a part of it. She grabs my hand and pulls me toward the door.

I'm not too concerned. Scuffles among the boys happen frequently and are usually resolved by the time I hear about them. But Maudine, our emotional 6-year-old, can't stand by and watch as the older children can. A fight just adds excitement to their day.

The first thing I see is Kenneth on his back in the dirt, crying and yelling "You just wait 'til I tell my daddy!"

James cowers beside the porch, more afraid of me than Kenneth's dad, I'm sure. After all, we agreed on the first day of school that fighting would bring punishment.

Visitor Unannounced

I listen as the others tell me what they witnessed. It does not surprise me that all but Margaret believe James is at fault. James can be an instigator of trouble, but Margaret is his neighbor and close friend.

Punishment is meted out to both boys. They will pick up trash, twigs, cones, whatever they find on the playground while everyone else has recess. James glares at Kenneth; Kenneth wipes his face on his sleeve, and we all take our places in the classroom.

Morning classes progress quite well until we hear a vehicle roll up at the front of the school. Everyone's head turns toward the door. It can't be the grocery truck stopping to sell us candy. It only comes on Fridays. My fear is that it is Junior, a young man who delivers fuel in the neighborhood, and who has asked me to go out with him. I have told him not to show up during the school day, but Junior has a mind of his own. Maybe it is Mr. George coming with treats for the children.

It isn't. It's Mr. Moore, the County School Superintendent.

"Good morning, class. Don't let me interrupt your lessons," he says.

Mr. Moore is a large, sandy-haired man, very professional in behavior and dress. I have only seen him twice. That was the day he called me out of the college classroom to interview me and the day I signed my contract. I was nervous those days, but today I am frightened out of my wits. Nobody told me the superintendent would come out to observe. I'll do what any thinking person would do. I'll pretend I don't know why he's here. I'll pretend to think he has dropped by to see how things are going, and to ask if we need anything. The children don't need to be a part of this, so I dismiss them for recess.

Mr. Moore and I have a friendly discussion. I assure him that I am pleased with the progress the students are making.

"Do you need anything that I may be able to get for you?" he asks.

"We need books on all reading levels for our library shelf," I reply.

"I'll see what I can do," he promises. "I'm glad to see that you are enjoying your first year of teaching."

Even if Mr. Moore had not known that this is my first year, he would guess it by the way I am acting, I think.

"Thank you for coming," I say as I ring the bell for the children to come in.

"Surely, I think I'll go down to the Negro school and see how they are doing."

How I wish for a way to warn my black friend down the road that the big boss is on his way. I can't, but then Mattie has been teaching for several years. She won't be flustered.

At the end of the day, I am reminded of the skirmish.

"Miss Beathard, you forgot to remind me and Kenneth to clean the schoolyard," James says with an angelic smile.

Visitor Unannounced

"Well, yes I did, but be assured, there will be another day."

The boys leave with a smile on their faces — good friends again.

Thank God for recess

CHAPTER TWELVE

Is There a Doctor in the House?

It is a cold and gloomy Monday. All of us mope in as we usually do after the weekend. Coats are hung in the cloakroom and lunches placed on a shelf.

I have printed a short story on the board using words familiar to the first graders. We read together, and individually, until they are reading it fluently. They search for and draw circles around certain words as I instruct. The other students do exercises from their spellers.

When we finish reading, I give Maudine and Kenneth a sheet with randomly placed numbers and instruct them to draw objects to match the numbers. While the upper grades work on their geography lessons, I work with the third and fourth graders on sentence structure and punctuation. English is my favorite subject to teach, so I try my best to make it fun for my students.

Is There a Doctor in the House?

In the middle of English class for the sixth through eighth graders, we hear a vehicle drive up out front. Who could it be this time?

"Happy Valentine's Day, kids — teacher, too!" Mr. George comes through the door with a sack in his hand and a grin on his face.

On Friday we cut out construction paper hearts and wrote silly verses on them to exchange as valentines this afternoon. But it seems we are going to have our little party now.

Mr. George passes out several little hearts to each one that read "Be Mine," "You're sweet," and stuff like that. Everyone begins reading them out loud. Occasionally one of the boys groans when his message is mushy.

"What does it say?" the girls ask.

"You'll never know," is usually the reply.

"Do you like candy?" Mr. George asks above the clatter.

"Yes sir," most reply.

"You bet we do," says James.

"Then hold your paws open." Mr. George walks up and down the short aisles, filling each hand with a variety of penny candy.

"And the teacher deserves something," he said as he places a five cent candy bar and a small box on my desk.

"Goodbye. Study hard," and Mr. George is gone.

I glance at the clock on the wall. It is lunchtime. "You may get your lunches," I tell the class, "and we may have another treat."

As the children spread their lunches on their desks, Miss Birdie walks in. She has a pot in her hand which she sets on the heater.

"Get your cups and line up. This hot cocoa should go well with your sandwiches on a cold day like this."

Miss Birdie had asked me this morning if bringing cocoa as a surprise would be okay. Of course, it will be a real treat, I told her. She stays to have lunch with Kenneth. I decide that since we are in a party mode, it will be a good time to let the children exchange their homemade valentines.

What an experience — lots of laughter, some teasing, some pretend angry slurs, but all in fun. Miss Birdie takes our cups out by the water bucket and gives them a good cleaning while we go out for a brief recess.

When I ring the bell for the afternoon session, all I can hear is "Do we h-a-f to come in?"

"Can't we do without 'rithmetic just for one day?" asks Margaret.

"Let us stay out and give us extra homework," George suggests.

"Heck no," says Clay. "Just be nice to us for once."

I debate the wisdom of it, but decide to give class a try. I assign everyone except the fourth, fifth and sixth grades work to do at their desks. George, Pearline, Margaret and Ada Jean are sent to the blackboard. I give each of them a problem

Is There a Doctor in the House?

appropriate to their level. George and Pearline are adding columns of five three-digit numbers. Margaret has a subtraction problem where borrowing is necessary. Ada Jean has a fairly simple multiplication task. I watch carefully to see what difficulty each has. George is doing well except for using his fingers to add. I step up beside Margaret to help her borrow from the tens column. Ada Jean is having trouble, too. She appears agitated.

"I'll help you in just a minute, Ada Jean," I say as I turn back to Margaret.

"O-o-o-o, Miss Beth…," Mable Clara stops in the middle of her sentence.

Something is wrong.

As she says it, Ada Jean is collapsing to the floor. She lies there with glazed eyes. I wonder if she is having a seizure.

What should I do?

Mable Clara runs for some water. I grab a handkerchief from my desk drawer, wet it and begin to bathe her face.

"Kenneth, you and George run to your house and get your dad. Tell him to bring the truck. Hurry!"

I lift Ada Jean's head and continue to bathe her face. After a long while, it seems, Ada Jean begins to stir. She looks around. It appears that she doesn't know where she is nor what has happened. Slowly we help her to her desk where she rests her head on her arms. It is frightening. She hasn't said a word.

Is she too embarrassed, or is she not aware yet?

Mr. Hand drives up and comes in. I explain what has happened and ask if he will take her home. I help get Ada Jean into his truck.

"Mr. Hand, I can't finish the afternoon." I am shaking all over, as if having a hard chill. I am nauseated.

"I can see that," he says. "Send the Marsh kids home, and I'll be back in a few minutes to take the others home."

"Thank you, class, for staying at your desks and being quiet. Ada Jean will be fine with some rest, I'm sure." I try to sound convincing.

"Put your books away. If you've finished your work, you'll have no homework. If not, try to complete it tonight. School is out for today. Those who walk may go. Mr. Hand will be back to take you others home. I'll see you tomorrow."

"I wonder 'bout that," I hear someone mumble.

A doctor in the house? That would have been nice — both for Ada Jean and for me. A party one hour and an emergency the next. As I walk home, aided by the fresh air, I think, that's just the way life is. Good times and difficult times. I need to work toward being better prepared for the bad times.

CHAPTER THIRTEEN

Teacher, I'm Bored

I never hear that in Bold Springs. There's no time to be bored. Besides, that word may not be in their vocabulary. Chickens have to be fed, pigs slopped and the cow milked, all before dark. Then homework! That never ending task.

When chores are done, kids in the family take turns riding the one bicycle they own. Or maybe, they kick a ball around and toward a designated goal, a crude game of soccer which none of them know anything about.

It is the same at school though more varied. On a nice day, marbles is a favorite game.

"You gals, smooth off a place in the shade," Bobby commands.

Mable Clara goes for the broom in the building and sweeps off the clumps of dirt, pine needles, cones, or whatever else that will interfere with the path of the marbles. Bobby draws a large circle on the cleared area.

"Throw in your marbles," says Bobby. "We'll take turns by age. I'll go first."

"Are we playing for keeps?" asks George.

"You know better than to ask," I tell him.

"Drat!" says James. "It's more fun to play for keeps."

"Not for the one that loses his marbles."

The game of marbles is not just for boys. The girls play too, but they have to be careful. They are in dresses. Occasionally one of the boys giggles and all heads turn toward the girls. In an instant each of the girls changes her position, wondering if her underwear is showing. It takes only once for the girls to react, to cause the boys to tease them with the giggling trick. The girls, however, can never be sure.

There is Mother May I, a group game that tests our concentration.

"Margaret, take one giant step and three baby steps," instructs Ada Jean.

Margaret leaps once and takes three tiny steps.

"Go back! go back!" we all yell. "You didn't say 'mother may I'."

Margaret pouts all the way back to the starting line.

Some days the lunch-time game is Piggy Wants a Signal. One person is "It" and hides his/her eyes. The others hide in view of the "pigpen," a circle drawn in the dirt. "It" counts to 20 and then opens his/her

Teacher, I'm Bored

eyes and goes about trying to find the others. When "It" finds one, the one found is put in the pigpen. She or he yells, "piggy wants a signal," then looks all around the schoolyard. When a hand or head is seen from behind a tree or bush, the "pig" can escape the pen and hide again. He or she has been given a signal. The game is over when all "pigs" are in the pen, or when "It" gives up.

Cops and Robbers and Cowboys and Indians are fun for the younger boys. No equipment is needed. Playing "cars" is a different story. They have no store-bought cars or trucks. At home, they use grandma's empty snuff bottles. These are four-sided bottles made of thick glass that won't break easily. At school, the boys create cars by taking half a hickory-nut shell and putting a marble or stone in it to identify its owner. Down on the ground, they sit or lie, pushing their cars along, making roads as they go.

While the boys play "boy games," the girls play Jacks or Pickup-Sticks, or paper dolls. The lunch hour is time enough to create a family from pages of a Sears Roebuck catalog, and make furniture for the family from cardboard or stiff paper.

As I said, I never hear a complaint about being bored. There is just too much to do.

But what about the teacher?

CHAPTER FOURTEEN

Life after Three-Thirty

"Hey Teach, there's a party at Eugene's place Friday night. You're goin' aren't you?" calls Son as he climbs off the school bus.

Son is Ada Jean's older brother. His real name is Eldon, I am told, but I never hear him called that.

"Sure, I'll be there, maybe with bells on," I call back.

About once a month someone in the community hosts what we call a "play" party. Teenagers and any single adults gather at a home, put a record on the old phonograph and each one grabs a partner. We prance around a circle similar to square dancing. Furniture usually has to be moved aside to make room. The fun really begins when one of the guys calls out instructions to a rousing tune.

"Swing your lady, then men turn back," and on and on until we run out of steam.

Life after Three-Thirty

We don't expect refreshments, but occasionally the lady of the house pops popcorn in the fireplace or on the wood-burning stove. Popcorn and a cup of hot cocoa on a chilly night are enough. Funny stories shared with friends make the evening one to remember. When we feel we've worn out our welcome, most of us head down the dirt road on foot, going home.

Bold Springs is not the most exciting place to be on weekends. With no car and no young people my age, I accept any invitation to socialize with people around me. Paying visits to my students' homes is not a good idea. No doubt, the kids would be ill at ease, maybe even frantic.

"What have I done now? What is my teacher telling Mama and Daddy?" They don't need the teacher hanging around after hours, so socializing with parents waits until after church services on Sunday.

The empty-nesters are a different bunch. Blanche and Edker's daughter left for Houston to work, so I have become a sort of surrogate family member to them. They invite me for meals often and to ride into town with them on weekends.

Eva and Big Mama are homebodies, but they love having visitors. At least once a week some of the Rogers family gathers at Eva's to play "42," a domino game known only to Texans, it seems. I am invited to join them.

"Shake a leg, gal. We're ready to play," Lewis Baker barks. He isn't being rude; he just has a booming voice.

In the game of "42", two players partner against two others. Each draws seven dominoes, then bids from 30 to 42, even 84, according to the dominoes drawn. The challenge is to observe what each player plays in turn, in order to hold a domino that might catch the high bidder's trick. Sometimes, deciding which domino to play takes me longer than Lewis thinks it should.

"Don't sit there, batting your eyelids like a bullfrog in a hailstorm," booms Lewis. "Lay one down."

My partner and I seldom win against Tub and Lewis, but, after all, they have played for many years; why shouldn't they win?

The deacons of the church, concerned about finances, announce in a Sunday service that we will have a box-supper the last Friday night of the month.

"Ladies, you know what to do. Decorate those boxes and fill them with tasty grub — and don't let your man see it! Did you hear? Don't let your man see your box!" Mr. George is emphatic. "And men, bring a full wallet. It's going to be a real dog-fight."

The day comes. I decorate a shoe box with purple crepe paper and glue on some yellow paper flowers. Miss Birdie fills it full of fried chicken, potato salad packed into small jelly jars, and puts in two of her fried pies. These are made from cooked, sweetened dried fruits, wrapped in Miss Birdie's flaky pastry, and deep fried.

Life after Three-Thirty

We all slip our boxes onto a table beside the pulpit. Every husband knows that he had better decide which box belongs to his wife and make the highest bid no matter what it costs him. Each begins with a low bid knowing that others will raise the bid. The evening becomes a dog-eat-dog party as Mr. George had said. Bidding stops when the men think a particular husband has bid his limit.

Bidding becomes fierce when the three teen-aged girls' boxes are held up. It doesn't seem to matter which girl belongs to which box. Either will be a prize, but five boys vying for three boxes is a sight to watch and hear. Occasionally, one of the girls' dads throws in a bid. That really adds fuel to the fire.

For some reason, my box is the last to be auctioned. My friend, Marvin, has driven out from town intending to win my attention.

"How much do I hear for this last pretty box?" asks the auctioneer. "Why, I think I'll bid five dollars. I'm hungry enough to eat a horse."

"Six dollars," Marvin calls out. Gracie whispered to him that the box was mine.

"Six and a half," shouts Tub.

"Seven," Marvin yells.

"Seven-fifty," calls Edker.

"Eight," said the auctioneer.

"Nine," retorts Edker.

Marvin has been laughing with the others during the competition, but now he looks worried. I hate to think of his driving the 10 miles out and not having a partner to share a meal.

"Ten dollars!" he shouts in desperation.

"It's sure a pretty box and heavy too," the auctioneer says. "Smells good too." He holds it close to his nose. "Do I hear eleven?"

Silence. Tub and Edker glance at each other and wink.

"Ten, going once, twice, three times and gone!" yells the auctioneer.

It is all over but the dining. Each guy opens his box, checks the name inside, and takes his lady to one of the 100-year-old pews. The teenagers head to the back corner where with some teasing, the lucky ones share with the two who don't have a box.

"I'm sorry they were so tough on you," I say to Marvin as I pick a spot on the steps to the podium.

"I knew it wouldn't be easy," says Marvin, "but when he asked for $11, I got troubled. Ten is all I had."

We enjoy our supper and laugh at the thought of those married men having two boxes of food to eat.

The deacons' idea for a box supper proves to be a great one. The church's coffer is enriched, and everyone goes home sufficiently stuffed and happy.

Play parties, dominoes, church and school activities, and then there were the quilting parties. About twice each month, the ladies gather at someone's home, usually Faye's or Gladys'. The furniture is rearranged to make room for a quilting frame to be set up. Each lady pulls a dining room chair up to the frame on which has been stretched a pieced quilt-top over the batting, and there they sit hours on end, sewing, and sewing, and sewing. All the while, each tells what she knows or has heard about everyone else in the community.

"Say, did you hear that Winnie's boy has gone to Texas A and M?"

"Naw! I always thought that boy would make something of himself."

"Too bad about the Jones girls. They don't have a grasshopper's chance at a decent future. Their old man won't let them out of his sight."

"I 'spect they'll run away the first chance they get."

"I would if I was them."

I am glad the quilting parties are during the day. At 19, I can't get interested and I have a good excuse not to participate. Besides, my presence likely would squelch their conversation. The time is well-spent, however, because the quilts are given to an orphans' home.

You get the picture. These are the kinds of activities that fill the spare time of the young and old in Bold Springs. This is our life, and most of us I imagine, never once think we are missing out on better things. To be honest though — I do occasionally wonder what my friends back in college are doing.

CHAPTER FIFTEEN

Follow the Leader

Lunchtime again. The children are anxious to get out of the warm and humid classroom. That is obvious by the way they slammed their books into the desks and rushed to get their lunches from the cloakroom.

Bobby usually latches on to the ball and bat as he escapes out the door. He is always first to claim a shady spot under a tree. The fastest four boys lean against the rough bark of the tree trunk, plunge their hands into their lunch sacks, and pull out a sandwich. It may be a breakfast biscuit with a sausage between halves, or perhaps a fried egg. Seldom is bread from a store-bought loaf seen. That is a luxury few in Bold Springs can afford. Besides, most families don't go into town often enough to have bakery bread.

Follow the Leader

Bobby is absent today. It is peculiar, I think, that Clay or George has not taken the ball and bat out, but soon I hear shouts that indicate other games are being played. Usually, I go out with the children at lunch hour. Today, I take two aspirins for stomach cramps, eat my lunch and spend the time checking papers and listening to the mid-day news and Glenn Miller recordings that follow.

"Let's play Follow the Leader, and I'm the leader," George yells from the playground.

"You boys are always the leader," says Margaret.

"We do better tricks. It's more fun with us leading," answers Clay.

That's a good idea. They can all play and there's not much chance of anyone getting hurt.

I hear them running and laughing as they circle the outhouses, jump over a log and shimmy as far up a tree trunk as they can.

"Good, the aspirins are doing their job, and I'll get these papers checked," I mutter aloud, not noticing that everything is suddenly quiet outside.

The music ends, commercials replace Glenn Miller and I remember. It is past time to ring the bell. Instead of going to the porch, I hold the bell out the window and shake it. Then I sit back down at my desk. Nothing happens. I hold the bell out the window again and ring it fiercely. I sit back down. Nothing happens — no footsteps, no voices, no one getting drinks on the front porch.

I take the bell and go outside. Could George have led them down to the spring? I wonder. But they could have heard the bell's ring at the spring.

My emotions begin to take over. I am concerned. Kidnapping is out of the question. That just doesn't happen in Bold Springs. Besides who would want nine more kids? But where are they?

On the front porch, I shake the bell long and hard. Mrs. Grimshaw can hear it from her pallet at her front door, I am sure. I will probably hear about it from her the next time I see her.

"Children, if you hear me, you'd better get into this classroom before I count to 10. One—two—."

I pause. No sign of movement on either side of the schoolyard.

"Three — four," I yell. As I begin "five," a quiet voice sounds from the cemetery across the road. One by one each of nine kids slips out from behind gravestones and heads back across the road to the school.

I am relieved. I go in and sit at my desk. I don't look up as each tiptoes in and sits down. My instinct is to laugh. I should compliment them for successfully playing such a clever trick on their teacher. But, I have to act angry, if for no other reason than to get back at them with a trick of my own.

When they are all seated, I walk to the corner and pick up my wooden paddle that stands there.

"George, you were the leader. You come stand facing the class."

Follow the Leader

"But, Miss Beath…" whispers George.

"No, 'buts' about it, George. You were their leader, weren't you?" I declare.

"Yes ma'am," George says.

One by one, I call each of them up to stand in a row in the front.

"Pearline, where are you to play at recess?"

"On the playground," Pearline answers.

"Margaret, what have all of you been told about the road?"

"Not ever to cross the road without you telling us we can," whimpers Margaret.

"Clay, what are you supposed to do when I ring the bell?"

"Get into the room lickety-split," answers Clay.

I hold up the paddle. "So which of you wants to be first?" I ask, in as stern a voice as I can muster.

Dead silence. All eyes stare straight ahead. No one moves.

"I'm the oldest," says Mable Clara. "I'll be first."

Mable Clara has witnessed a few paddlings before. She knows the routine. She bravely walks to the end of the desk, bends across it, and braces herself with her hands.

I raise the paddle to administer the first lick. Eight gasps come in unison from the row of children standing like stone statues.

That does it. I can't pretend any longer. I put the paddle down, give Mable Clara a pat on her rear, and say, "Each of you get back to your desks, and don't ever give me a scare like that again!"

Seconds seem like minutes before they realize I am laughing. Hesitantly, one by one, they begin to laugh as well. Then I hear James say, "And don't you ever scare us like that again."

CHAPTER SIXTEEN

Easter in the Park

This year an Easter egg hunt is our spring outing. The children look forward to a half-day off on Friday. The weather isn't much of a concern even though Easter comes in March. A rain shower, if one comes, will pass quickly and the sun will break through the clouds.

The children take care of the Friday chores in record time. George and James grab the erasers to dust them on the old tree stump outside. Bobby washes the blackboard with a little help from Maudine, and the girls sweep the classroom and empty the pencil sharpener. Clay and Kenneth sprint down to the spring to pull out any twigs and leaves that have fallen in. They dip out as much of the water as they can to rid the spring of any insects that have fallen in, then rush back with the pail full of clean, cool water.

We wash our hands after closing the windows and door, and are on our way. Some have baskets. Others carry paper bags that they have decorated.

In a matter of minutes, we arrive at the place where the ladies are waiting. Bold Springs has no park with mowed grass, landscaped flowerbeds and groomed bushes, so the mothers have chosen an open area in a pasture behind the Hands' place. Each has brought a dozen or so decorated, boiled eggs to hide. They place eggs under broken tree branches, on fallen logs, in bushes, behind stones, and even in the lower branches of trees. Blanche and several other ladies who have no children in school join in the fun. The ladies have prepared a picnic lunch, as well, for us all to enjoy.

Lunch is already spread on a quilt on the ground. Each of us chooses a sandwich and a cookie, then finds a place to sit. Extra sandwiches and cookies are not extra for long. The kids see no reason for leftovers, so with permission, they finish them off.

When our stomachs feel satisfied, Miss Birdie explains the boundaries within which the eggs hide. In unison the ladies count one, two, three, go! And the kids are off.

"Here's one," someone yells

"I found one!" Maudine screeches.

We hear cries of excitement all around for a long time. Finally, one by one, they come back to the group.

Bobby has held back most of the time. After all, he is too old for such childish things, he had said back at school. But while we are counting everyone's booty, Bobby wanders out to find all that have been missed.

We count 99 that have been found.

Maudine has the fewest, only seven. Clay has the most — 16. There is a rumor going around that Clay's Aunt Pearl gave him subtle hints as to where he might find eggs. I have to admit that I think the rumor believable.

"There are only 99 eggs here," Miss Birdie announces. "That means there are 21 out there somewhere."

"No, only 10 missing," Bobby calls. "I have 11."

All the while we are hunting eggs, the black crows are in a dither in the trees around us. They seem to resent our retrieving anything from their territory and are telling us so.

Miss Birdie looks up. "Okay! Okay!" she says, apparently addressing the crows. "You can have what's left, if you can beat the squirrels and armadillos to them. We need to be on our way home."

The sun is getting low in the sky and the March winds are cooler. Everyone picks up his bag or basket and turns toward the road.

"Thank you, for the party," Margaret says to the ladies. She gives Clay a disgruntled look and walks in the opposite direction. Margaret's mother is not here.

"You're welcome," several mothers reply. "See you Sunday."

The Spring—Our water supply—Fifty years later

CHAPTER SEVENTEEN

Naiveté at Its Utmost

"Confession is good for the soul." Isn't that what the Bible says somewhere among its pages? Well, my soul needs some "goodness," so here goes.

As I look back, I cannot believe Sandy Moore, the County School Superintendent, has kept me as an employee three years. I cannot believe that all the parents of these students have trusted me to teach their children these years. He has, and they have, and amazingly we all are surviving.

I've admitted how unprepared I am for bloody incidents, and for fainting episodes. There is more.

"Miss Beathard! Miss Beathard! James stepped on a snake and it bit him." George yells from the direction of the spring.

"What happened?" I ask as two excited boys get to the porch. George is carrying a half-full bucket of drinking water. James is partly hopping and partly walking on his heels. I set him down and look at the bottom of his feet. Somewhere I have learned, or at least heard, that a snake bite leaves three puncture marks in a triangular shape. There they are, three red marks on James' foot.

Now what do I do? There's no way I can cut an X on those spots to suck the venom out. Besides I have nothing to cut with. Send him to Mr. Hand, Kenneth's dad.

"Kenneth, you go with James and George and ask your daddy to take a look. He'll know what to do," I say with some conviction.

The boys hurry off, James still on his heels. The remaining ones of us go on with our activities halfheartedly.

More quickly than I can imagine, the boys come rushing back into the classroom. "He's okay! It's not a snakebite. James probably stepped on a sweet-gum ball," Kenneth announces.

Praise the Lord. If it had been a snake bite, especially by a rattler, James would be lying along the hot, sandy road, dead.

There is more.

"Who were the friends you were visiting with in that big black Buick at noon today?" Tub asks. Tub Rogers is one of my school trustees.

Oh my gosh! He saw me in that car in the churchyard.

"Not friends," I reply. "Two fellows trying to sell me some life insurance. I wanted to hear them out since I don't have insurance of any kind. It was unbearably hot, so they suggested we sit in the car under a shade tree across from the playground. I could still watch the kids playing while looking at the materials." I ramble on, attempting to explain away my embarrassment and stupidity. "I didn't sign up — I told them I'd consider it."

"It has been a scorcher," Tub says and walks away.

I think I have met my Waterloo. If Tub ever mentions it again; or if the insurance salesmen come back, I may be in trouble.

Needless to say, I have a lot of maturing to do.

CHAPTER EIGHTEEN

A Lesson Learned

Spring is a beautiful season in Texas. It begins in February and turns to summer by the end of April. Redbud bushes and white dogwoods, heavy with blossoms, stand out among the leafing trees and towering pines. Purple violets creep up among the decaying debris in the wooded areas.

The large windows are open and cool breezes drift through the classroom. Birds of many colors and sizes warble happy tunes, sprinkled with the harsh cries of the crows.

What can put a damper on such a day as this in our little classroom? Absolutely nothing.

We decide that when our morning's tasks are done, we will take a nature walk back into Mr. George's pasture. What insects are stirring? Are tadpoles frisking around in the pond? What wildflowers can we find? There is much to learn as we go.

A Lesson Learned

"Put your materials away," I tell the class. "We'll walk down to the gate, spend about a half-hour searching, then come back for lunch."

"Why don't we climb through the fence and save time?" George asks.

"Well, if each of you feels comfortable climbing under the barbed wire, we can do that."

"The question is, can you climb under the wire, Miss Beathard?" asks Bobby. "The rest of us can." Nothing would please him more than seeing me caught on a barb halfway through.

"Of course, I can," I reply. "Let's go."

We take a shortcut to the edge of the pasture. I hold the second strand of wire up for each to climb through. The girls go first, then the boys. All of them continue walking.

"Hey! Who's going to hold the wire for me?" I yell.

"Oh," says Bobby. "We didn't know you'd need help, too. Do you trust me?"

"Do I have a choice?" Midst giggles, and with a silly grin on his face, he comes back to help me crawl through.

It is fun to get away from the building. The pond teems with tadpoles. Insects are everywhere — waterbugs, ants, a caterpillar. A turtle suns itself on a fallen log. The girls show more interest in picking wild flowers to take back to the classroom.

All too soon, it is noon. We are hungry and thirsty. "Come on kids. Let's go. We are fairly close to the gate, so we'll leave through it. I don't want to chance being left in the pasture."

"Do you think we'd do that to YOU, Miss Beathard?" George quips.

"Yep, we would," says Clay.

I give him a surprised look. Everyone laughs. I move toward him looking as vicious as I know how.

Clay hurriedly moves away. "Okay! Okay! Just joking," he yells.

The boys run on ahead to the school. As they get to the school yard, they begin screaming.

Another catastrophe? Not today!

"Get away! Go! Get out of here!" They all shout at once. Each boy darts here and there yelling. "You beasts! Thieves! We'll kill you!"

I can't imagine, but soon we know. Mrs. Grimshaw's hogs have visited the school as they often do. But this time, since no one was around, they ventured into the building. In the cloakroom, our lunches were more than they could resist. Three hogs are picnicking outside in the shade of the porch. Two others feast inside.

The shouting drives them out and away. All that is left is a mess of ripped paper bags and waxed paper.

"Do we laugh, or cry?" Margaret asks. "What are we going to eat for lunch? I'm hungry."

Everyone, except Maudine, laughs to think that hogs have played this trick on us. Maudine doesn't see anything funny about it.

A Lesson Learned

"Those mean old hogs!" she says as she begins to cry.

Ada Jean comforts her with, "Teacher will think of something."

But what? I decide to send Bobby and Kenneth down the road to tell Mrs. Grimshaw what has happened. What can she do about it now? I question. But it seems to ease the minds of the others.

We gather the garbage, then begin playing "Mother May I." In just a few minutes, it seems, Kenneth, Bobby and Mrs. Grimshaw walk up.

"Go wash your hands, kids," Mrs. Grimshaw commands. She is carrying a large paper bag. Bobby holds a glass jug of milk.

We do as we are told — no questions asked. Mrs. Grimshaw puts a peanut butter sandwich made with store-bought bread and a cookie on each desk. Bobby pours milk in each child's cup.

What a feast! And what a sweet thing for Mrs. Grimshaw to do. The children seem to forget that Mrs. Grimshaw is usually scolding them for chasing her hogs and jumping on them.

They don't like her much because she is nearly always grumpy; but today she is an angel.

An art teacher, I am not, but I decide the best plan for the remaining hour will be art. I instruct the children to write a sentence or two telling what they learned from our nature walk today and to draw a picture related to it. I print Maudine's and Kenneth's stories for them.

Maudine draws a bouquet of flowers; Kenneth, the turtle on the log. James draws the teacher climbing through the fence. Margaret's picture is of violets with a bee on one.

I am not surprised when I read on six of the papers: "I learned to shut the door when we leave the building."

Homework will be light this evening. No time for it. By the time the children tell of all the excitement of the day, it will be bedtime.

What next? I wonder.

Miss Donna's hogs—Regular visitors

CHAPTER NINETEEN

Bethel Baptist, The Center of Our Community

Bethel Baptist Church was organized in 1849 with seven charter members. By 1861, there were 71 white members and 31 Negro slaves. The pews in the church were constructed by the slaves. Soon after the Civil War ended, the Negroes organized a church of their own up the road.

The church has an interesting history. Minutes of the business meetings of the church have been preserved through most, if not all those years. Brothers and sisters of the church were expected to live pure and moral lives. If they didn't and were found out, they could expect a visit from a discipline committee from the church. They either came before the congregation and confessed and repented, or the congregation withdrew fellowship from them.

In May, 1905, two men were appointed to talk to Brother John Smith (name changed to protect the guilty) about his drinking and using profane language. Brother John told the committee, "I won't come before the church until other brethren sweep around their back doors." He didn't, and the church dismissed him from membership.

Women were not exempt from church discipline either. The two sisters Bennett (name changed) were seen dancing and received a visit by a committee. The committee reported back to the church on June 1, 1905, that the two sisters were sorry they had violated the rules of the church and that they did not want to be turned out. They were forgiven.

Most interesting is the claim by Brother John Smith in July of that year, that he wasn't aware that any committee had confronted him, and that he had been turned out "without a chance."

H—mm, could it be that he was too inebriated when the visitors came to remember their visit, or maybe the committee of two men needed to "sweep around their doors," and didn't confront Brother John?

At any rate, Brother Smith asked forgiveness for his wrong living, and was received back into the fellowship.

There came a time in the church's history when the swine presented a problem. The Grimshaw hog families, and who knows whose others, liked to root around under the church building. I suppose it was cooler under there.

Monday through Saturday, nobody cared. On Sundays they were a dreaded nuisance. Their grunts and squeals did not fit in with the preacher's sermon.

Bethel Baptist, The Center of Our Community

The deacons had to do something. The solution — they fenced the animals out by stretching wire around the foundation of the building. Skunks and other unwanted varmints could still get under, however, so that presented another problem, a horrendous odor when one died under there.

When I arrived in September, 1948, Brother Moore was pastor and had been for several years. He, his wife, and two daughters, 12-year-old Gracie and 4-year-old Judy, came from Leggett two Sundays each month.

Everyone in most households is up and dressed in his Sunday best and on time for worship at eleven o'clock. Much of the time, I direct the song service. I choose the old hymns that we all know, but some like what are called southern gospel songs, so we scatter in a few spirited songs like "I'll Fly Away" and "I've Got a Home in Gloryland." Young Gracie is our accompanist and she is a master of them all.

The pastor preaches at least a 30-minute sermon, then we sing another song during which everyone, not already a member and a professing Christian, is invited to come forward to talk with him.

When the last "amen" is said, we all head to a little side room where the ladies spread a meal fit for a king. It is traditional that we share a meal after each morning service. Chicken and dumplings, fried chicken, potato salad, vegetables from the gardens, and pies and cakes galore — we can't wish for anything different.

Soon we are all sufficiently satisfied, sometimes miserably so and we go back into the sanctuary for a second service. This is done so that those who come from a distance will not have to return at night, and to give farmers time for their evening chores. By three o'clock, we are free to take an afternoon nap, or gather for a game of dominoes, or just sit in the porch swing at home and watch the world go by.

Funerals are always at the church and burial in the cemetery beside it. Weddings in the church are few and far between. No one can afford them. When a couple wants to get married, they go to the preacher's home or invite him to theirs. Then friends and family gather for a very informal reception before sending the couple off, usually to Houston or Galveston, for a brief honeymoon. The bride and her groom are happy with the attention paid them. They don't know any other way.

It is true; everything in Bold Springs revolves around the church and the school.

CHAPTER TWENTY

One Day at a Time

"Clay, leave me alone. Stop it!" James is yelling at the top of his voice.

I hurry out to find Clay and Kenneth, each with one of James' arms, attempting to wrap him around the hickory tree. James' face is pushed against the rough bark.

"Clay! Kenneth! Get inside and into your seats. You'll spend your lunch hour with me." I am furious. Such bullying is happening too often. Sending a note home with Kenneth might have some effect on his behavior, but I doubt that a note will serve any purpose with Clay.

Clay stomps into the classroom but not until he grumbles, "I'll get him, just wait." Kenneth follows. I can tell Kenneth is afraid of what may happen next.

I check James' arms and face. He has no apparent wounds.

"I wish I didn't have to come to school," James says, his lips quivering. "They're always pickin' on me. I'm scared."

"Yes, James, I'm beginning to notice. Are you sure that you aren't doing something to provoke them?"

"No! I don't do nothin' to them. Clay is just mean, George too."

From the beginning of the year, it has been obvious to me there is division in the community. It is as if the school and church are an imaginary line separating the two halves. Those on the south side, though poor, seem to think of themselves as less poor, more motivated, and better equipped for life's challenges than those up the road. They have "normal" families, a mother, a daddy and kids. Most have a vehicle of some kind, own their homes, have beds to sleep on, and a radio to gather around at night for entertainment. A cat or two and a big mongrel dog wander around the sheds or curl up on the porch. These are necessary — the cats to catch the rats and the dog to chase away varmints from the chicken coop.

For whatever reason, the kids from the north side of school are not so advantaged. They come from more transient families. Some are living with grandparents; some have step-fathers or no fathers at all. They live in small, old, rented houses off the

One Day at a Time

dirt road. Their clothes are made from printed feed sacks — some of mine are also — and several don't own a pair of shoes that can keep the grass-burrs off their feet, or the mud from between their toes. Their lot in life has, no doubt, caused them to be meek, less confident, unsure of their worth. And they, James, Margaret, and the Thomason sisters, are most often the objects of the bullying.

I send the remaining eight off to play, assuring them that this kind of behavior is not acceptable and will not be tolerated. How to stop it, however, is a monstrous question in my mind; *go to the parents, get the instigators and victims together, face to face, and hope they can find a solution among themselves, or what?*

In the classroom, I sit at my desk glaring at Clay and Kenneth. After a few, long minutes, I speak.

"Boys, what gives you the right to torture James?"

Clay jumps at the opportunity to speak. "Miss Beathard, we were only playing. We didn't hurt him, wasn't goin' to. James is such a sissy, a crybaby."

"Playing or not, James asked you to leave him alone, and that should have been the end of the game. I can't make you boys like James, and I certainly won't try to make James like you; but, this 'playing,' as you call it, must stop."

"We promise. We won't bother James again this whole day," announces Clay. Kenneth nods in agreement.

"This day, tomorrow, and the next day," I proclaim. "And if you do, it will be a cold day in July, before you have any free time. Do you understand?"

"That must mean never," Clay says.

"You are so right."

It is time to ring the bell to end the lunch hour. Eight children come in quietly after getting a drink on the porch. Their eyes are on Kenneth and Clay. Clay returns the gaze with an "I dare you" look. Kenneth doesn't look up.

We plunge into arithmetic lessons. Everyone has assigned exercises to do while I work with each grade on whatever new concept that needs to be introduced. Bobby isn't getting along well with decimals, nor is Ada Jean with fractions. Mable Clara has both down pat, so she works with Maudine and Kenneth. They are learning to recognize coins and their values. Maudine can't believe that having two nickels is better than having six pennies. She probably hasn't handled many coins in her lifetime.

We finish the day with geography. Then, before I dismiss them for the day, we have a discussion about respect — respect for one another and for another's property. Discussion? It is more of a lecture. I am still upset by what happened. And to make matters worse, Margaret overheard Clay and George talking of a plan to "get" James with a knife in the toilet. She said she thought I should know.

Lord, this is SCARY. Why are these boys even thinking of this kind of behavior? It's a sure thing

I won't get much sleep tonight. I'll have to figure a way to deal with that tomorrow.

"You aren't gonna tell Mama are you?" Kenneth asks before he leaves for home.

"I'll have to think about that, Kenneth. It depends."

CHAPTER TWENTY ONE

The Worst of the Bad

Everyone came in at the first ring of the bell. The boys looked so innocent. Perhaps our little talk about respect has served its purpose.

We say the pledge, sing "America," and I open the Bible to 1 John 4:20-21.

"Who will volunteer to read our Bible verse this morning?" I ask.

Silence.

"I will," Mable Clara says.

She reads it slowly and clearly. "Whoever loves God also loves his brother."

"Now, we'll say the Lord's Prayer together," I say. We do, then plunge into our reading lessons.

While working with Kenneth and Maudine, I stop and ask, "Do any of you boys have a knife? I need one."

The Worst of the Bad

No one does and no one asks why I need one. Thank goodness, because I really don't. I'm not sure what I would have said had they asked, but my anxiety level drops several notches. James is safe, I think.

Morning recess goes smoothly — no fights, no injuries. James and Margaret bring cool water from the spring. There is a marble game in the shade of a tree. The girls play on the swings and see-saw.

"I'm glad we had no problems on the playground this morning," I say when recess is over. "We all have more fun when we respect each other. Agree?"

Heads nod. We alternate our spelling lessons with reading about clouds and the weather associated with each, then have a group discussion about it.

It is lunch time. I am pleased about how productive the morning has been. The heat of the day drives us all outside in search of a cool breeze. The girls gather around a concrete block behind the school.

Trading items from the lunch bags is a common practice, especially among the girls. Ada Jean's mother is noted for her homemade sausage which she sandwiches between biscuit halves. Margaret has salmon patties in her lunch regularly, and Mable Clara has light bread and Spam. Each thinks the others' lunches are tastier, so if Ada Jean brings two sausage sandwiches, she has a Spam sandwich and a salmon patty to enjoy.

When I ring the bell to end the lunch period, the boys habitually dash water over their faces and run wet hands through their hair to cool off. They play hard and are hot, sweaty and stinky. The girls keep their distance from them.

We begin arithmetic. After giving instructions to all grades, I call Clay and James up to the blackboard. I have not noticed that James' desk is empty.

"Where is James?" I ask.

"He was on the playground," Kenneth answers.

"Maybe he is still at the toilet," Clay says.

"Bobby, will you go find James?"

Bobby is soon back in the room, his fingers clamped over his nose.

"Miss Beathard, James needs you on the porch," Bobby says.

"Oh."

Several kids start to the door.

"Sit down! James needs me, not you."

James is standing at the bottom step. His pant legs are wet and dirty up to his knees. He is crying and angry. And he smells, and not of sweat.

"James, where have you been? What happened?" There is no way I could have been prepared to hear what I hear.

"I've been in the toilet, Miss Beathard. Can't you tell? Clay and George came in while I was sitting on the hole. They picked me up and pushed me down in there," James tells me.

I can't believe it, but the evidence is there. James' arms are red and scratched where he hurt them getting out.

The Worst of the Bad

"James, I'm so sorry. I want you to go home to get clean, but I want you to wait here a few minutes."

I come back into the room, angrier than the proverbial bull seeing red. I jerk Clay by the arm, pull him to the front and lean him across my desk. I grab my wooden paddle from the corner, yell "Clay Wallace Lawrence, grab the side of the desk with both hands," and I give him the paddling of his life — maybe the only one he's ever had.

Clay screams "Don't hit me again! I'm sorry! That hurts!"

"That's exactly what I intend," I say. I don't count the number of swats I give him, but it is enough.

"George, take your place at my desk."

I don't expect George to cry out. He is too obstinate to let his peers think he is hurting. I give him the same consequence, several hard licks with the paddle and send him to his seat in tears.

"Both you boys stay after school," I say. "I intend to write your daddies a note."

I go to the door. James is still standing there waiting.

"Go on home James, and tell your parents what happened. I'll see you tomorrow."

We finish our lessons for the day.

"We have a new rule," I say before I dismiss the class. "There will be only ONE person in either toilet at a time."

Those in charge of cleaning finish their tasks. The others leave for home. Clay and George sit.

I take my time writing notes to the parents. Finally, I give George his note.

"By the way, don't believe I won't know if your daddies don't get these. George, you may go."

"What about me?" Clay asks.

"In a while," I answer.

When I think that George has reached the cut-off to his house, I give Clay his note and excuse him. In a few minutes, I look up the road. Clay is running as fast as he can toward home.

Surely I have seen it all. Tomorrow has to be better.

CHAPTER TWENTY TWO

Wheels at Last

Some of my new friends at Bold Springs are amazed that I am content walking the mile or further to school after I moved to Faye Rogers' home the second year. It is a long walk on cold rainy days. It isn't lonely because the Marsh children join me each morning, but sometimes it is scary.

Cows, some with long horns, and an occasional big bull graze along the road. Even Bobby and George walk softly as we pass. None of us needs to be reminded that the animals were there first. The road is their turf. It is free range country.

Walking is not my first choice, but at this time it is my only choice. I don't know how to drive, have no car to drive, and don't have money to buy one. Those are reasons enough, I think, but Edker and Blanche don't think so. They decide that Edker should teach me to drive. Since the pump-station where Edker works is across the road from the

Rogers' place, it is convenient for him to get me in the driver's seat and have me drive him home and have dinner with them and then drive back. Edker's car is a nice, almost new Chrysler and easy to drive except when the roads are rutty. By the end of the school year I am confident that I can pass the test for a driver's license.

At home in Huntsville this summer, I visit my good friends, Jeff and Jeannette.

"You know, Jeff, I think I'm brave enough to try for a driver's license."

"Well, it's about time! Are you planning to use your dad's car?" Jeff asks.

"Guess so. Is there a problem?"

"There might be," Jeff says. "His is an old, well-used car, and might not pass inspection. They'll be checking the lights and brakes. It's safe for your dad because he's used to it, but it might not be for you."

"H-mmm. So?" I mutter.

"Jeannette, what do you think of letting Frankie use our car? I could ride with her to the courthouse and wait for her to finish the test."

"That's a great idea," Jeannette replies. "You're free tomorrow morning." So it is arranged.

Jeff picks me up this morning; actually he has me drive. What a friend! He waits for me to take my written test and my vision examination, then sits with me until I am called for the driving test.

Everything goes well until I'm told to parallel park. I pull forward, back and turn, pull forward, back and turn, pull forward, back and turn. Finally the officer says "Let's go back to the courthouse."

I get my license in spite of the parking. Jeff is waiting to take me home. When I tell him about my dilemma, he laughs.

"Why worry? Neither Huntsville's nor Livingston's streets are marked for parallel parking, and for sure you won't be parallel parking in Bold Springs. Now if you'll be driving in Houston...."

"Not a chance!" I interrupt. "I'm not that crazy."

Before the summer is over, Daddy approaches me about taking his car, an old '37 Plymouth. He knows of another one that he can get.

We agree on a price. I pack my few belongings and head back to my little community. Driving along by myself in my own car, I feel special. I am really independent now. At last, I'm a grown-up. I have a job and a car. What else can I want?

I sing to myself and enjoy the sights as I pass through Phelps, Oakhurst, Point Blank, Onalaska and Kickapoo. Forty-five miles from Huntsville, I reach Livingston.

I need to share my joy with someone, so I drive by Wayne's and Roland's house. Luckily, I find them home. They are glad to see me, and thrilled about my car, they say.

After a short visit, I head up the highway north of town and turn onto the dirt road to Bold Springs.

Reality strikes. I have to cross the railroad tracks where there is no signal. The tracks run across the top of an incline. I stop the car, shift into a lower gear and creep up the slope looking in both directions. Safely across, I begin to worry about the bridge across Long Cane Creek. The bridge is built of timbers laid crosswise with two by twelve runners the length of the bridge on both sides. The idea is to drive your wheels up on those runners and stay on them until you cross to the other side. The bridge is long and high above the creek, and has no rails. It is hair-raising to say the least.

Again, I stop the car, shift into low gear and ease onto the runners. When I am sure all wheels are where they need to be, I grip the steering wheel with both hands, stare at the runners with my good eye, and hope for the best. Minutes later I am on the good earth again and feeling relief. The driver of the car waiting to cross on the other side probably is relieved as well. The bridge is a one-way crossing.

Faye, Tub, and their daughter, Bobbye Lee, welcome me home. They help me unpack the Ford, then leave to take Bobbye Lee to her boarding house in town for her senior year in high school. After my belongings are put away, it's time to write a postcard to Mama and Daddy to assure them that I crossed Long Cane safely.

Labor Day, 1950, my routine begins again almost the same as on the last two Labor Days — getting my school building ready for my kids. My wheels make the difference.

Wheels at Last

My wheels

CHAPTER TWENTY THREE

The Upside of Teaching

Teaching in the 1940s is an honorable profession. We are respected and appreciated.

Parents are grateful for our efforts to help their children and support our decisions. When "Johnny" is disruptive in school or disrespectful and is punished, he can look forward to consequences at home. That is my experience in Bold Springs at least, and from talking with friends in other districts, they agree.

The salaries are not to boast about, but for me, a single white female, mine is okay. I am paid $160 a month. Sad but true, my black friend up the road only makes about 70 percent of that. Male teachers can expect at least one third more, but our elite counterparts in town are paid even more. Why the difference? We accept it as fact, rather than protesting. Our contract states that we are not to be paid

The Upside of Teaching

for sick days. My trustees must not have reported my sick days, although mine are usually sick partial days, because my salary has never been docked.

During my second and third year in Bold Springs, I have boarded with Tub and Faye Rogers. My car payment is flexible, but I regularly pay $30 each month. Having been taught that at least 10 percent of what I make belongs to God's work, my fixed expenses are these:

$16 to church
$40 for room and board
$30 for car payment
$86 total

That leaves me with plenty for gas, clothes, personal necessities and some for saving. A nice dress can be bought for $6 or $8. Shoes are not special to me. Two pair are all I need, and I can buy a pair for $6 or less. What a life! I have no complaints.

With my savings, besides paying college expenses in the summer, I was able to buy my mother an old upright piano to replace the one she had to leave when they moved to Huntsville.

In addition to my teaching salary, there are other benefits. Since I am the only single lady in the community, several young men have vied for my attention. One was a banker's son who was in medical school. Had I cultivated that relationship, I might not have this story to write, but he came on too strong and too fast. One date was enough for me.

Another was a friend from college who drove over one night unexpectedly. Faye met him at the door and told him that I had gone into town to spend the weekend with Wayne. Faye laughed as she told me later of his reaction. He was stunned and speechless, and as he turned to leave, she explained that Wayne was a married lady and a good friend.

"Go on into town. Frankie and Wayne will be glad to see you," Faye told him.

"Are you sure?"

"Yes, I'm sure. I'll give you directions."

It was a pleasant surprise to see him and we enjoyed the evening, Wayne, her husband Roland, little Tommy, and Travis and I.

Every so often the propane fuel truck that supplies the farms in our community shows up at the school. Junior drives it and somehow his schedule usually puts him in the vicinity of the school at lunch time. He'll come onto the porch, sit on the rail, and visit. His rump hangs off the rail and is too much of a temptation for the children to resist. They make a game of slipping up behind and pitching small stones at his backside. Junior responds with a friendly threat.

Junior came by one wintry afternoon. "A group of us are driving down to New Orleans for Mardi Gras next weekend. Would you like to go with us?" he asked.

A picture of gloom and doom flashed before me. I saw a car wrapped around a light pole and me lying in a ditch. All I have heard about Mardi Gras is that hundreds revel in the streets, drunk and out of their conscious minds, and I could picture Junior and his friends among them.

"No," I said. "Thanks, but I have plans for the weekend." *Shampooing my hair, trimming my toe nails, finishing report cards — those are plans, aren't they?*

Another friend, Marvin, lives in town with his dad. His mother has died. He is sort of a jack-of-all-trades. He repairs cars and heavy equipment. He owns a bulldozer that pushes down bushes and small trees, so he picks up odd jobs clearing land.

Marvin is a friend "who sticketh closer than a brother." He is the first to notice a strange knock in the old Plymouth's engine and he takes care of it. He takes me places when he senses that I don't want to drive alone. One night Marvin literally saved my life.

He had insisted on driving his car ahead of me to be sure that I got back to Bold Springs safely. My headlights had been acting up. As we approached the summit of the large berm on which the train tracks run, Marvin applied his brakes with force. It startled me, but I was able to stop. Just then a freight train rumbled through the crossing. Marvin had seen it and could have crossed over, but he knew that I would follow.

His car stopped just feet from the tracks. I was saved. Marvin is, as we say in East Texas, "a good ole boy," with grease under his nails, and a gentleman.

The visits and attention of these young men help to break the monotony of rural life for me, and probably give the quilters topics of discussion. The children take notice of certain cars and trucks passing their houses and headed in my direction, and bring it to my attention in a teasing way on Monday mornings.

"Miss Beathard, whadju do Saturday night?"

"Not much," I say.

"Yeah, well I saw Marvin's car headed down toward Mr. Tub's place," Clay says.

"Yeah, and it stopped there," George adds. Tub's house is in sight of George's house.

One thing is for sure. There are no secrets in rural East Texas.

1951: One lone young lady among the boys

CHAPTER TWENTY-FOUR

The End of the Ride

"School's out! School's out!" yells Kenneth.

"No more homework!" Clay whoops.

"Don't have to tote no more buckets of water from the spring," mumbles Ada Jean.

Since she and Pearline saw the black panther run up the hill from the spring on one of her trips to get water, Ada Jean hasn't been happy with that assignment.

I tolerate their joy, but I am close to tears. Pretending to be glad it's over is far from easy.

During this third year, we were joined by two brothers new to the community. Bobby Glass and his younger brother, Carl, came to live with their uncle Ed Baker. Bobby Marsh and Mable Clara are already in high school, so for a short while, we were a family of 10 again.

Bobby Glass is a gentle, industrious sixth grader in bib overalls with a captivating smile. Carl, a cute, not so gentle, third grader most often is described by his classmates as "mean." I have the impression that school is a safe haven and pleasant experience compared to their family situation. Perhaps at least Bobby is sad like me to see the school year end.

"Goodbye. Have a great summer. Read a lot and practice arithmetic so you'll be ready for school in town. I know you're going to love it."

"What are you going to do now, Miss Beathard?" asks Ada Jean.

"I'll be sitting in classrooms and doing homework all year as you will; in fact, my classes begin in two weeks. Don't you feel empathy for me?"

"What's empathy?" Ada Jean asks.

"Oh, that's a grown-up word. You'll find out soon enough."

I look forward to getting back in college, but it hurts to think of leaving. Pearline and Maudine are not with us anymore. Their mother took them to a neighboring town to live — physical abuse, I hear. Since Margaret's mother died, her dad moved to find work. I miss those girls. Ada Jean does too. She has been the only girl for several months. The seven who remain will be bussed into Livingston. I may never know how they do and what they will choose to do with their lives. My hope is that I've made a difference in this community; that they are ready for what lies ahead.

The End of the Ride

I hug them all. The boys are mortified, but to get out the door, they surrender.

I give the rooms a little touch of cleaning. As I organize the textbooks on the shelf in the cloakroom, my mind turns flip-flops.

How many hands have held these same books? The school has been here 50 years that I know of. What books were used before these texts were published? What will happen to this building? Have I taught these children enough that they can do well in town? Will they adjust well to large classes and single grades? Are they disciplined enough to make it in their new environment?

After three years my life is changing. The school year has ended. The school is being closed for good. I've had three beautiful, rewarding years with these kids. I've made friends that will be forever friends. With summer classes behind me, I have one final year of college before getting my degree, and I have had three years of experience as a teacher.

Back to reality. I need to collect my belongings and get home, so I clean out the desk drawers. Washington and Lincoln are still peering down at me. The flag still stands in the corner. It seems fitting to leave the Bible and the bell on the desk. I close the windows. With blurred eyes, I shut the door behind me, crawl into my old jalopy, and head to Faye's house. Faye's house has been my home these last two years. As I turn the corner by Miss Birdie's house, I wave to Kenneth and Clay playing in her front yard. Almost home, I pass the Marsh house and honk. Mr. Tom Marsh is sitting on his porch. He waves.

Miss Gladys invited me to supper this evening. I hurriedly freshen up and change from my sweaty clothes to a loose sleeveless dress and slip on my sandals. I drive up her lane just at six o'clock. Mr. Wainwright likes to eat at six and I am hungry.

We feast on ribs, creamed potatoes, and greens with big chunks of turnips in them. Cornbread muffins and iced tea complement the meal. A cruet of vinegar and a bottle of pepper sauce, along with butter, sit in the center of the table. Of course, a white starched tablecloth with pink roses embroidered at the corners graces the table. Gladys' whole house is spotless and homey with handmade decorations everywhere — lace curtains and crocheted doilies, and flowers from her yard. Stuffed animals perch in chairs and on the floor.

Pictures of her son-in-law and two grandchildren, and of her daughter who died, hang on the walls on both sides of the fireplace.

The three of us sit around the table after eating and visit. Miss Gladys puts away the leftovers.

"I think I hear a knock at the door. I'll check," Mr. Wainright says.

Before we know it, the living room is filled with almost every lady in the community. Each of them carries a package wrapped with lovely paper and ribbon. Some of them are wrapped, I notice, in wedding type paper.

What is going on?

The End of the Ride

I am told where to sit.

"We hope someday you'll find the perfect man, and we thought we'd start a hope chest for you," Faye explains..

Blanche laughs. "You ran off Travis and Marvin. Junior didn't have a chance, then lo and behold, you gave your engagement ring back to Carl," she reminds me. "But we aren't giving up on you."

Surprised and on an emotional trip, I begin opening gifts. Everything has been made by hand or at least decorated by hand. Beautiful embroidered dresser scarves are from Faye. Gladys has embroidered pillow cases. Both these ladies had tatted lace around the edges. There were appliqued kitchen towels, aprons, bath towels with crocheted trim — so many beautiful and thoughtful gifts. I can't forget these friends even if I wanted to. Mrs. Grimshaw has come too. That makes the evening extra special. It will be hard to sleep tonight.

Today is Saturday. Tub, Faye and I have a scrumptious breakfast.

While Faye does dishes, I pack my belongings and clothes, and of course, my gifts, and Tub helps me load my car.

Mr. George came to say goodbye. After he'd gone I found a note that had been slipped under my door. It was from Mr. George. It said, "I want you to sing at my funeral." I smile and wonder, will I even know when he dies?

On purpose, I put on my grubbiest clothes this morning. I know packing and unpacking the old car will be a dirty job. Besides, I am just going home, my real home, in Huntsville. Mama and Daddy won't care how I look. They will be glad to see me even in rags. Actually my slacks do have a tear at the knee, and my blouse has a bottom button missing. I don't care and no one else will either.

Wrong. I go up the hill to say goodbye to Big Mama Rogers and Eva. They walk down the length of the dog-trot and out onto the porch as I drive up.

Big Mama takes one quick glance and says, "Child, are you going out of here looking like that?"

"Yes ma'am. I'm just going home. I'll be there in an hour and a half."

"Well, child, I hope you have car trouble and everybody in the county sees you like that."

The three of us have a good laugh. I am glad it is not a sad farewell.

I drive off, honking the horn in front of the houses as I go until I am out of Bold Springs and headed toward Onalaska. About 8 miles up that dirt road, I hear and feel, thud, thud, thud, thud. A tire is flat and I don't have tools to change it; wouldn't know how anyway.

As I walk in the hot noonday sun, three miles into Onalaska, to get help, I have to smile.

Big Mama Rogers is getting the last laugh. Her wish has come true.

CHAPTER TWENTY FIVE

Epilogue: Where Are They Now?

I retired in 1993, after 25 years doing what I had said I'd never do. As I said goodbye to my last class, a class of 25 kindergartners in Oregon. I was overcome with nostalgia.

I thought of Ray and Noel, first graders in West Texas, of Isaiah, a fourth grader in Houston, Willie, a first grader in Michigan, Johnny in kindergarten in Oregon, and many others. I thought of 25 years with an average of 25 children each year — 625 lives I had touched, and wondered if I had done all that I could for each of them. I concluded that if I had helped one each year, my efforts had been worth it, my time well spent.

My mind then sent me back to Bold Springs and the 12 who left footprints on my heart in those early years. I vowed on that day I would find them and renew relationships. Now in 2005, with help from

Clay and Margaret, I've visited with all of them, personally or by phone, except one. Carl Glass died this spring, 2005, of a heart condition. I am sad that I didn't find him sooner.

Where are those kids now? The roll call of the Bold Springs School for the years 1948 to 1951 looks like this in 2005:

Kenneth Hand and his wife, Caroline, live in Livingston, Texas. Until he was disabled by a brain tumor, he worked as the assistant manager of an auto parts department. They have two children. Kenneth remembers the teacher living at his house and the fun times on the playground.

Maudine Thomason Jackson and her husband live in Murchison, Texas. She has three children — and horses and mules. Maudine remembers that I gave her the only spanking she ever received in school, after which I gave her a piece of cake. She knew why she got the spanking, but she didn't understand about the cake. I do; it was my conscience getting to me.

Clay Lawrence and wife, Marsha, live in the home he grew up in at Bold Springs. He was a carpenter and floor installer. He has three children.

Clay remembers the Christmas plays and receiving a nice gift. He admits to his part in putting the armadillo in the girls' toilet. He also remembers the times the teacher got sick at school and sent the children home early.

Clay remembers the bell, also. So sure that one he found at a barn sale was the bell from our

Epilogue: Where Are They Now?

classroom, he bought it, cleaned it, and gave it to me when I visited the community a year or so ago. Bless his heart.

James Hudson and wife live in Goodrich, Texas. He was a professional wrestler, and later a cross-country truck driver. He has two children.

James remembers the toilet incident — how could he forget? He remembers the Easter picnic and egg hunt, but little else that was pleasant since he was the object of most of the teasing. James does remember his "very good teacher." Thanks, James.

Pearline Thomason Hensley lived in Reading, Pennsylvania many years. Her truck driver husband was transferred there from East Texas. This summer they moved home to Onalaska. They have 10 children.

Pearlene recalls going to the spring with Ada Jean and hearing the panther nearby. "It sounded like a lady screaming." The girls dropped the bucket and ran as fast as they could back to the building. After that, the big boys were sent for water. Pearline remembers going to the fair in Mr. George's pickup. He had put hay in the bed of the truck to make the ride more comfortable. Mr. George thought of everything.

George Marsh and wife, Marie, live in Bold Springs, just feet away from his childhood home. He worked for Sam Houston Electric Company 27 years. They have two daughters.

George recalls out-running Carl who was chasing him with a brick. He didn't remember shoving

James down the toilet hole, but said, "If he says I did, then I probably did."

Margaret Coker Woolf and husband live in Livingston, Texas. She married when still in her teens. She has five children. Margaret was afraid to go to the toilet. She expected to find spiders, praying mantises, and maybe even a snake in there. She remembers the Halloween activities especially, because she won a cake.

Ada Jean Chalker Davenport lives with her husband on the Bold Springs road. She has four children. Ada Jean recalls that I was the first teacher who didn't take the class to funerals that were held in the church across the road. "To be respectful, you made us stay inside the school-building," she reminded me. "Walking to school was scary. There were cows everywhere." She remembers the day that a hickory nut fell from the tree and hit her head.

Bobby Glass was a long-distance truck driver and a heavy equipment operator associated with the Ogletree Corporation. He is also an ordained minister. He and his wife of 47 years live in Moscow, Texas. They have three children.

Bobby liked school because "I wasn't having to pick cotton or gather corn." Bobby also remembers picking violets in the springtime. He was nicknamed Twinkle Toes. He thinks it was because he didn't have any shoes.

Epilogue: Where Are They Now?

Mable Clara Marsh Sloan and her husband live in Channelview, Texas. They have two children.

"You seemed more like a sister to me than a teacher," Mable Clara told me. She remembers riding with me in the old Plymouth to Onalaska to play ball with other kids on weekends. She enjoyed the times I let her work with the young ones. Believe me, I was grateful for her help.

Bobby Marsh lost his wife in 2004. He lives in Highlands, Texas, near his two children. He was in a management position with Crown Zellerbach for many years. Bob is a music enthusiast, singing and playing guitar in a band. He admits to having had a "crush" on his teacher. I didn't know.

Most of my students live within a stone's throw of the community where they grew up. They range in age from 63 to 70 years. All have fond memories of their years at Bold Springs School. They have done well, even though none were privileged to go to college. I'm pleased to know, however, that many of their children did. Some even chose teaching as a career.

I am so grateful to have had a small part in the lives of these 12, and all the others, and so blessed with the memories.

"Thank you, Lord. I DID enjoy the journey."

WHAT ABOUT THE SCHOOL BUILDING?

What happened to it? Exactly what should have happened. Since the school and church were the heart of the community, it was only fitting that it be joined to the church building as its fellowship hall. Services are now held every Sunday and tradition lingers. The original pews are still used, and lunches are still spread after morning services, but only once a month.

The lifeblood of the community—Bold Springs School and Bethel Baptist Church—United

To order additional copies of

Ten Kids *and* A Teacher

Please visit our web site at
www.pleasantword.com

Also available at:
www.amazon.com
and
www.barnesandnoble.com

Printed in the United States
139597LV00001B/69/A